'There are only about 20 murders a year in London, and not
husbands killing their wives.' *Commander Hatherl*

'Men must go ahead . . . women must follow, as it we
D. H. Lawrence

'Margaret Thatcher is doing for monetarism what the Boston Strangler did for
door-to-door salesmen' *Denis Healey*

'The only woman in the world who can kick-start a jumbo jet' *An Australian newsman
on 'Big Marj' Whitlam*

'A woman's place is in the wrong' *James Thurber*

*M*en live up to their reputation for bitchiness in this hard-hitting collection of funny stories
and one-liners that take for granted the superiority of the male sex. Mothers-in-law, women
drivers and Mrs Thatcher are just a few of the traditional targets for the acid tongues of
writers, actors, politicians and media men from Aristotle to Winston Churchill and Les
Dawson.

Illustrated by Bill Belcher

This book is dedicated to Lynne,
for all my inhumanity to her . . .

Copyright © Graham Jones 1986

First published in 1986 by Century Hutchinson Ltd,
Brookmount House, 62–65 Chandos Place, Covent Garden,
London WC2N 4NW

Century Hutchinson Publishing Group (Australia) Pty Ltd,
16–22 Church Street, Hawthorn, Melbourne, Victoria 3122

Century Hutchinson Group (NZ) Ltd,
32–34 View Road, PO Box 40–086, Glenfield, Auckland 10

Century Hutchinson Group (SA) Pty Ltd,
PO Box 337, Bergvlei 2012, South Africa

Set in Linotron Sabon Roman and Bold by
Rowland Phototypesetting Ltd,
Bury St Edmunds, Suffolk
Printed and bound in Great Britain by
R. J. Acford Ltd, Chichester, Sussex

British Library Cataloguing in Publication Data
Jones, Graham, 1951–
   I don't hate men but . . . I don't hate
   women but . . .
   1. Sex —— Anecdotes, facetiae, satire,
   etc.
   I. Title
   306.7'0207   HQ23
   ISBN 0-7126-1205-X

Designed by Gwyn Lewis

I DON'T HATE WOMEN, BUT...

Graham Jones

CENTURY   LONDON · MELBOURNE · AUCKLAND · JOHANNESBURG

Contents

Preface
The Patron Saint of Male Chauvinism

Salimbene, the thirteenth-century Franciscan, was the greatest collector of anti-female brickbats:

> Wouldst thou define or know what woman is? She is glittering mud, a stinking rose, sweet poison, ever leaning towards that which is forbidden her.

> Man hath three joys—promise, wisdom and glory: which three things are overthrown and ruined by a woman's art.

> Lo, woman is the head of sin, a weapon of the devil, expulsion from paradise, master of guilt, corruption of the ancient law.

> Woman is adamant, pitch, buckthorn, a rough thistle, a clinging burr, a stinging wasp, a burning nettle.

Not to mention:

> Where woman are with men, there shall be no shortage of the Devil's birdlime.

THAT'S MY FINAL OFFER. THREE TWELVE-YEAR OLD VIRGINS FOR YOUR ROTTEN DONKEY

1 Man's Inhumanity to Woman

Of all the plagues with which the world is curst,
Of every ill, a woman is the worst.
George Granville, Lord Lansdowne

'It's a man's world', as the old saying goes, and men have been trying to prove it for centuries.

> Woman is a pitfall—a pitfall, a hole, a ditch.
> *Anonymous Mesopotamian poet*

> Woman! The very name's a crime.
> *Robert Gould, eighteenth-century satirist*

> This triform monster . . . it is blemished with the belly of a reeking kid, and beweaponed with the virulent tail of a viper.
> *Walter Map, twelfth century*

> Women are like elephants to me: I like to look at them, but I wouldn't want to own one.
> *W. C. Fields*

> Woman are like flies: they settle on sugar or shit.
> *Truman Capote, 'Mojave'*

> They have a right to work wherever they want to—as long as they have dinner ready when you get home.
> *John Wayne*

> I like women in their place. I like them on their knees in the kitchen, doing the dusting or whatever. In return I feed them, wine them, make them laugh, and give them a punch on the nose and a good kicking when they need it.
> *Oliver Reed*

> If you saw women getting out of bed in the morning, you would find them more repulsive than monkeys. That is why they shut themselves up and refuse to be seen by a man; old hags and a troupe of servant-maids as ugly as their mistress

surround her, plastering her unhappy face with a variety of medicaments. For a woman just does not wash away her sleepiness with cold water, and proceed with a serious day's work. No, innumerable concoctions in the way of salves are used to brighten her unpleasing complexion.
> *Juvenal, Roman satirist*

*P*olitics is the arena where the self-protection club of male dominance is guaranteed to strike at any up-and-coming dame:
> **So tough she could kick a bear to death with her bare feet.**
>> *Colorado politician on Anne Burford, Environmental Protection Agency chief, before she was ousted*

> **The only woman in the world who can kick-start a jumbo jet.**
>> *Australian newsman on 'Big Marj' Whitlam*

Mind you, her husband was prone to a little chauvinist piggery himself, stunning the wives of Commonwealth heads of state with the immortal:
> **I've always fancied a slice of black tart myself.**

*B*ut when it comes to provoking some good old male animosity, nobody is quite in the same league as Britain's Margaret Thatcher:
> **The Dolly Parton of British politics.**
>> *Julian Barnes*

> **A latter-day Winston Churchill in drag.**
>> *Denis Healey*

> **There isn't one leading British institution she can resist looking closely at—and then hitting with her handbag.**
>> *Peter Hennessy*

*M*ind you, some female members of the Royal family have run Mrs T rather close:
> Her Royal Haughtiness . . . has failed her mother and failed the country.
>> *Harry Arnold, royal newsman, on Princess Anne*

> The Royal floozie.
>> *Willie Hamilton on Princess Margaret*

> Why shouldn't she have the common touch? She is one of the most common-looking women I've seen in a long time.
>> *Taki (Peter Theodoracopulos), columnist, on Princess Beatrix of the Netherlands*

*T*he word 'woman' is itself the very embodiment of male chauvinism, for it comes from the Anglo-Saxon 'wifman', meaning 'wife-man'. The implication, then, is that there's no such thing as a woman separate from wifehood.

But we all know how men love and cherish their espoused.

> A wife is classed with the greatest evils.
> *St Jerome*

> If you are really devoted to one woman, then bow your head and yield to the yoke.
> *Juvenal*

If nothing else, 'the wife' might give you a laugh.

> I wouldn't say she's fat, but she hung up her bra in the desert and a camel made love to it.
> *Les Dawson*

> My wife went to a horror film and the audience thought she was making a personal appearance.
> *Les Dawson again*

*M*ind you, there's another side to the coin that can be witnessed at any divorce court.

A German wife went to the divorce courts claiming mental cruelty. She said her chief pleasure in life came from reading detective novels. But every time she bought a new one, her husband would write the name of the murderer at the head of Chapter One.

A Connecticut woman got a divorce when her husband made her sleep with a squirrel when he was away on business.

And a Chicago man applied for a divorce of the grounds that his wife was not able to take a single trick in a card game, although she had 13 diamonds.

Then there was the incredible case where a husband's curly toe-nails led to divorce. Mrs Margaret Bruce, 51, was granted a decree in the London divorce court after Judge Roger Gray, QC, heard that science-teacher Reginald Bruce, 64, had not trimmed his toenails for nine years. According to his sister-in-law they curled around his feet and reached his ankles. Said the judge: 'It offended his wife. I think it would have offended any other wife.'

*O*f course, some sex warriors take things even further.

> No man is fit to be called a sportsman who doesn't kick his wife out of bed on average once in three weeks.
> *R. S. Surtees, English squire*

> Certain women should be struck regularly, like gongs.
> *Noël Coward, 'Private Lives'*

William Sheraton, 34, gave his wife a black eye for serving up a too-flat Yorkshire pudding. He preferred them the way his mother made them, Barnsley magistrates heard. When his wife Joan served them on Sunday, he complained they were not thick enough. There was an argument and he struck her in the face, blackening her eye. He pleaded guilty to assault and was bound over to keep the peace for 12 months. Later, at his home, Mr Sheraton said: 'In my opinion the Yorkshire puddings were too thin. They were like ice-cream wafers.'

*J*ohn Marshall of Omaha, Nebraska, promised his wife Lea just before her birthday in 1984 that he would not tell anyone when she reached 50. So he put an announcement in the local paper, adding that 'in deference to her age' he would say no more. But on her birthday he threw a party. Under a banner reading 'Lea Marshall is 50 years old, old, old', 20 friends were there to chant: '50, 50, 50.' In the swimming-pool there was a huge foam cake . . . with 50 candles. The cruel husband had even hired a plane to fly overhead trailing the message: 'Lea Marshall is 50 years old, old, old.'

An Austrian farmer offered his best customers a free gift in the summer of 1983. Anyone who bought ten sacks of potatoes got a free romp with the farmer's wife.

Magistrates at Taunton, Somerset, heard in 1983 how jobless Bernard Sowden had beaten up his wife—with a dead rabbit. After hitting her around the head with the rather stiff doe he then hurled her into the air. He was bound over to keep the peace.

*I*n August, 1985, a master at Mons Comprehensive School, Dudley, West Midlands, decided to test whether male chauvinism was still alive by asking a group of 15-year-old boys to complete the sentence: 'A woman is . . .'

WHAT DO YOU SEE IN LITTLE ME?

GIVE ME A MOMENT. I'LL THINK OF SOMETHING

The answers were malicious. 'Scum that paints her face . . .', 'something to be kicked when you're drunk . . .', 'a thing to beat about the house . . .', 'an ugly thing that increases population . . .', 'a thing to use for clearing away the beer cans'.

There's no hiding place from male chauvinism, even in outer space. When Soviet woman cosmonaut Svetlana Savitskaya began her first day's work on board the Russian space station Salyut, she found herself on the receiving end of some not very 21st-century jokes. 'We've got an apron ready for you, Sveta,' said flight-engineer Valentin Lebedev in a film shown on Soviet TV. 'It's as if you've come home. We have a kitchen for you.'

Showbusiness, like politics, seems to bring out the most offensive side of the male psyche. Yes, this is *real* sex war. Man as superbitch.

> **The face that launched a thousand dredgers.**
> *Jack de Manio on Glenda Jackson*

> **No one has done such harm to Anglo-American relations since George III.**
> *Peter Ackroyd, British TV critic, on Joan Collins*

> **She is to acting what the *Titanic* was to safety at sea.**
> *Taki on Farrah Fawcett-Majors*

When he was drama editor of the *New York Times*, ace wit George S. Kaufman was once asked by a press agent: 'How do I get our leading lady's name in your newspaper?' He replied:

> Shoot her.

Tatum O'Neal once arrived at a glittering Los Angeles party for Ken Russell, wearing a slithery silver evening gown and silver glitter eyelids. One of her male hosts ungallantly greeted her with:

> How amusing. You've come as a baked potato.

But, as Richard Savage (*c.*1697–1743) said:

> Such, Polly, are your sex—
> Part truth, part fiction;
> Some thought, much whim
> And all contradiction.

George Meredith (1828–1909) was equally cool:

> I expect that woman will be the last thing civilized by man.

Rudyard Kipling (1865–1936) ? Well . . . few could ever forget:

> A woman is only a woman,
> But a good cigar is a smoke.

2 Vultures! Man's View of Woman through the Ages

Woman is by nature inferior to man: therefore she must obey . . .
Aristotle

There is nothing in the world worse than a woman, save some other woman.
Euripides

There are three kinds of women: the beautiful, the intelligent, and the majority.
Anonymous

Men, some to business, some to pleasure take.
But every woman is at heart a rake.
Alexander Pope

Women are one and all a set of vultures.
Petronius, first century AD

Woman is frail, and proclive unto all evils . . . a very weak vessel.
Hugh Latimer

God created Adam lord of all living creatures, but Eve spoiled it all.
Martin Luther

There is a tide in the affairs of women which, taken at the flood, leads—God knows where.
Lord Byron

Men are women's playthings: women are the devil's.
Victor Hugo

Woman begins by resisting a man's advances and ends by blocking his retreat.
Oscar Wilde

There's nothing so similar to one poodle dog as another poodle dog, and that goes for women, too.
Pablo Picasso

Men are better at everything . . . You don't kneel to women, you mistrust them.
Rudolph Nureyev

A woman's place is in the wrong.
James Thurber

Most women are just average—egotistical, avaricious, spiteful, mean and argumentative.
Peter Cagney

Of course you can't trust women—they all want to be wives.
John Wayne

3 I'm No Woman-Hater, But...

I'm not a woman-hater. Life is only long enough to allow even an
energetic man to hate one woman—adequately.
Frank Richardson, 2835 Mayfair

The latest research by American sociologists throws an intriguing new light onto just how much men actually do dislike women. E. E. Lemasters found that the ordinary man does actually 'prefer men as a species to women . . . except for sexual purposes, he finds women dull and uninteresting'. Edgar Gregerson studied insults in more than 100 languages and found far more directed against females, or using the names of female parts of the body; and Connie Eble (author of *If Women Weren't Present, I'd Tell You What I Really Think*) proved there are actually more ways of insulting women than men, as well as more animal terms for women.

Yes. It's an unchivalrous world.

Police who were called to the home of a married couple in Leeds, Yorkshire, found the wife locked in a chains wrapped around her neck and then made to form a chastity belt.

Husband Lyn Roland Buckley, 24, a store manager, pleaded guilty in June 1974 to assaulting his wife Pamela, causing her actual bodily harm, not to mention unlawfully conducting himself in a noisy, disorderly and turbulent manner to the annoyance of his wife.

When the police had come, he had handed over the key to a padlock allowing her to be freed and said: 'I have to bring her in line every now and then. When she's been chained up she's a different woman.'

Richard Gere was once asked by a young female reporter from *Ladies Home Journal*: 'What's it like being a sex symbol?'

The ungallant star responded by dropping his trousers.

The reporter maintained her composure. She said in a matter of fact way: 'I've seen better', and carried on with the interview.

On the Dick Cavett show, the host asked Chad Everett, star of *Medical Center*, whether he had any pets. 'I have six animals,' said the TV star. 'Two dogs, three cats, and a wife.' A fellow-guest, comedienne Lily Tomalin, an ardent feminist, was so incensed she walked off the show.

*S*pecial prizes for insensitivity to spouses must go to: HENRY KISSINGER, who for his honeymoon with Nancy in Acapulco, invited Hollywood impresario Robert Evans along for company; JOHN F. KENNEDY, who in the early years of his marriage to Jackie, decided she was a political minus, and told her: 'The American people just aren't ready for someone like you. I guess we'll just have to run you through subliminally in one of those quick flash TV spots so no one will notice'; and, perhaps most insensitive of the lot, England soccer international FRANK WORTHINGTON who, when invited by a sports journalist to name his 'most dangerous opponent', shot back: 'The wife.'

*A*ctor James Caan has hardly shown himself the most gallant male in Hollywood with real-life lines like 'Stay away from me girls, don't beg' and 'Sure I liked her. Had her, didn't I?' Costarring with Lauren Hutton in *The Gambler*, he became so frustrated with her acting that he said: 'Johnny Weissmuller had it easier than me. I'll give you a banana every time you get it right.' Then, true to his word, he brought 20 pounds of bananas onto the set, giving her one every time the director yelled 'Print!'

On Sally Kellerman, his costar in *Slither*, he said:

> I couldn't stand to kiss her. I got some bubble gum. It came time to kiss her, I stopped everything and said, 'Wait a minute, gotta get rid of this.' The next take, when I was supposed to kiss her, I yelled, 'Stunt check.' But they wouldn't give me a stunt man so I had to do it.

My nomination for champion misogynist of the music business is Michael Jackson. Ensconced with a menagerie of two fawns, a sheep, a brace of cockatoos, an eight-foot boa constrictor called 'Muscles' and a llama called 'Louis' (whose party piece was to do tricks like walking on its knees), he told in April 1983, how:

> I like them better than girls. They don't talk back.

*T*V-am chat-host Nick Owen scored a low blow for male chauvinism the day he asked actress Joanna Lumley if she were wearing any knickers. (Can you imagine the reaction if Angela Rippon had asked a male guest that question?)

> There's about as much charm to her as there is to the kind of woman you see driving buses or wielding pickaxes.
> *Simon Winchester, on the election of Mayor Jane Byrne*

When Maureen Colquhoun MP made it to the British House of Commons, a male colleague sauntered up and told her how very pleased to see her in the House. Looking at her seriously he said: 'Now you'll be able to do something about the food in this place.'

*N*oël Coward was not one to disguise a deep-seated misogynistic 'bent'. When watching in New York a film of the Coronation of Queen Elizabeth II, his fellow guests were most impressed by the sight of the gigantic beaming frame of Queen Salote of Tonga. One friend remarked: 'She's wonderful. But who is the little guy sitting up front in her carriage?'

'That,' said Coward, 'is her lunch.'

> The sensible executive fits office sex into *his* schedule, at his convenience, rather than allowing it to disrupt the orderly routine of life. I know a man who always asks his secretary to sleep with him. Some do, some do not. When he finds one who will sleep with him, he takes her then and there on the surface of his desk, arguing that a certain brutality and swiftness of approach establishes him from the beginning as the person who is in control . . . At the first sign of 'involvement', the suggestion from the woman that it might be nice to go out for a drink or to have dinner together, he finds her a new job and fires her.
>
> *Michael Korda, 'Male Chauvinism—How it Works'*

*M*ore insensitivity Oscars: PETER O'TOOLE, who once at the Château Marmont Hotel in Hollywood rushed around shouting 'Fire! Fire!' for the satisfaction of forcing a pretty young girl to stand shivering semi-nude on the pavement outside.

Hollywood mogul JACK WARNER, who, raising his glass at the end of a lavish banquet attended by Madame Chiang Kai-shek said, to embarrassed silence: 'Madame, I have only one thing to say to you—No Ticket, No Laundry.'

And JUDGE THOMAS KELLOCK QC, who in February 1985 warned an Old Bailey jury not to discuss the case before them with their families. He then added: 'But speaking for myself, I don't find it that easy to tell my wife to shut up.'

*M*en also refuse to take bigamy seriously, despite the suffering it may cause:

> Sir—One wonders why, after having 105 wives, Mr Giovanni Viglotto should be sentenced in Pheonix, Arizona, to 34 years in jail. Hasn't he suffered enough?
> *Letter in 'Daily Telegraph'*

> Is not the trial a waste of time, for the verdict is obvious? Any man who marries 105 times has to be guilty of bigamy. But insane.
> *Philip Wrack, 'News of the World'*

4 Savage Put-Downs

The last time I saw her she reminded me of Rider Haggard's
Ayesha after one trip too many through the Fire of Eternal
Life—hairless, shrivelled, and black as a tinker's nutting bag.
Auberon Waugh on Olga Deterding

*H*ell hath no fury like a *woman* scorned? In the sex wars, when it comes to real bitchery, you can't beat a man for sheer, undiluted vitriol. With woman the target, of course.

She has the commanding glacial presence of a female Rommel.
William Marshall, 'Daily Mirror', on Julie Andrews

When hosting a programme featuring singer Helen Reddy, Las Vegas talk-show host Dick Maurice remarked to his listeners that 'success in show business boils down to having 10 per cent talent and 85 per cent ambition'.

The following night US comic Pat Cooper appeared on the show and announced: 'Helen Reddy is absolutely right and I couldn't agree with her more. She does only have 10 per cent talent.'

His words started one of the hottest showbiz feuds for years.

*W*hen introduced to Linda McCartney, wife of Beatle Paul, comedian Norman Gunston cut her down with:

It's funny you know, you don't look Japanese . . .

Perhaps one of the best put-downs ever, though, came from Maurice Gibb of the Bee Gees. Asked by an interviewer about his wild lifestyle, he replied:

One magazine said I went around smashing up Aston Martins. But that was when I was married to Lulu.

*S*ome more five-star cutting comments:

Cilla Black
The only person I know with two backs.
Frankie Howerd

Barbara Castle

I see this preposterous woman only as a persecutor of the self-employed . . . She has failed in her job and should now be sent to prison like any other 63-year-old hooligan.

Auberon Waugh

Joan Collins

She only smokes cigarettes after making love—and she's down to two packs a day.

Dean Martin

Britt Ekland

Her voice sounds like a duck flying backwards.

Ex-boyfriend Simon Turner

Julie Goodyear

She looks like a particularly nasty road accident.

Anonymous male critic

Vicki Hodge

This aging, raddled blonde . . . not only has a reputation that would make most sensible men turn and run a mile. She also has the kind of horse face that would keep them running.

Sir John Junor, 'Sunday Express'

Sue Lawley

. . . She is *the* plain Jane.

Chris Greenwood, 'Sunday' magazine

Heather Locklear (Sammy Jo of *Dynasty*)

The one with the neon teeth and a bottom like an under-ripe satsuma.

Stafford Hildred, 'Daily Star'

Madonna

Comparing Marilyn Monroe with Madonna is like comparing Raquel Welch with the back of a bus.

Boy George

Georgia O'Keefe

I wouldn't pay 25 cents to spit on a Georgia O'Keefe painting. So arrogant, so sure of herself. I'm sure she's carrying a dildo in her purse.

Truman Capote

Elaine Paige

She looked extraordinarily like Princess Margaret, which, if we had been going to do a film about the Royal Family would have been fine . . . I thought that if dear old Barbara Windsor dies, which heaven forbid, and we come to make the Barbara Windsor story, then Elaine would be perfect for the role.

Ken Russell

Victoria Principal

She has the sort of sex appeal that makes men want to jump into bed . . . turn over, and go to sleep.

Simon Kinnersley, 'Sunday' magazine

She's about as sexy as a 10-gallon hat full of Horlicks. As much of a turn-on as having ice emptied down your trousers. She's about as alluring as Hilda Ogden the morning after a heavy night at the Rovers Return.
Simon Kinnersley again

Nancy Reagan

Her favourite junk-food is caviar.
John Carson

Her smile could unseat an injun at 100 paces.
John Wayne

Angela Rippon

I've seen better legs on a Yank racehorse.
Boston TV critic

Diana Ross

She looks like a walking blood clot.
Frank Sinatra, on her dazzling red party dress

Meryl Streep

A creep. She looks like a chicken—she's got a nose like a chicken and a mouth like one.
Truman Capote

Margaret Trudeau

I don't go out with housewives. I never have, I'm never going to.
Mick Jagger

Raquel Welch

The world's first plastic woman.
Hollywood wit

5 Favourite Targets for Male Bludgeons, Blunderbusses and Brickbats: Show Business

Actresses will happen in the best regulated families.
Oliver Herford

*S*ome women are just naturals for the male sex-war offensive. Their glittering success unleashing the crudest and darkest in masculine envy.

With her tarantula eyelashes and constant near-hysteria there is something intensely irritating about Liza Minnelli.
John Blake, 'The Sun'

That chunky little sexless bundle with the massive bosoms and hair like a hayfield after a rainstorm.
William Marshall, 'Daily Mirror', London, on Bette Midler

During my romantic scenes with her I had to think of my pet dog to take my mind off what I was doing.
Co-star Ken Wahl, also on Bette Midler

It's tougher still on the way up. Betty (Lauren) Bacall had just graduated from the American Academy of Dramatic Arts and was trying to make an impression on Broadway. She marched up to one famous producer and announced proudly: 'Hi, I'm an actress.'

He looked her up and down and replied: 'My dear, the disguise is perfect.'

*B*arbra Streisand certainly worked her way up to become one of the most publicly despised women in showbusiness. If the occupational hazard for an actor is falling in love with his leading lady, the occupational hazard for working with Barbra is, to hear her leading men talk, a coronary, a nervous breakdown or a quick exit to the funny farm.

Can all the stories be true? Barbra Streisand has throughout her career been on the receiving end of male sniping because of her

unconventional looks. She's been called
Ant eater
The Big Beak
Ugly Duckling
Crazy Barbra
Her face, they say, is like
a Russian wolf-hound's
a myopic gazelle's
a furious hamster's
She's been called
the funniest ugly girl in the world
the ugliest funny girl in the world
And even
McEnroe with music

*E*lliott Gould said he married her only because 'she had a great apartment over a fish shop'. James Caan, at a London press conference publicizing *Funny Lady*, said: 'I've got to get out of here. She's driving me bananas. She's crazy.' And Robert Redford, too, rather ruined his usual screen image as a man of breeding and distinction when, after his fall-out with Barbra during the filming of *The Way We Were* (they weren't speaking by the end of the film), he took off for a basketball game rather than watch the premiere.

But it was during the filming of *A Star is Born* that the sparks really flew. Barbra's time on the set with Kris Kristofferson was described as 'like a rehearsal for World War Three'. Perhaps the most bitter fight between the two was heard by 40,000 amazed extras. They had arrived to be the 'audience' for a scene at an outdoor rock concert but, instead of music blasting through the giant speakers, they heard a vicious slanging match. Someone had left the microphones on by mistake.

Kristofferson, of course, blamed Streisand. He said, 'Filming with Streisand is an experience which may have cured me of movies,' and added: 'Working with her is worse than being in an army training camp.'

Said the *New York Post* at the glittering Christmas premiere: 'She isn't content merely to upstage her own movie—she wants to upstage God himself.'

*R*aquel Welch has been on the receiving end of some intense male chauvinism because her famous looks have tended to eclipse her acting ability. When she told the director of *One Million Years BC* that she'd 'been thinking about' one scene he replied:
Thinking? What do you mean you've been thinking? Just run from this rock to that rock, that's all we need from you.

When moves were afoot in Monaco to try to have Princess Grace canonized as a saint, there was a none-too-kind response from Hollywood. Said one tinseltown figure: 'But Grace never performed a miracle.' Then he added, as if in triumph: 'Oh no, I'm wrong. She did win an Oscar.'

*F*rom saints to apparent sinners. Jane Fonda's smooth progress to Hollywood superstardom in the 1970s was matched by an equally effortless and equally meteoric rise—to become the most abused, most vilified woman in America. Among the more polite nicknames she acquired for her off-screen anti-Vietnam-war activities were

>Hanoi Jane
>Commie Slut
>Red Pinko
>The Mouthy Twerp
>Hanoi Hannah

Robert Steele said she was

>A spoiled brat who doesn't know what she's talking about.

William Buckley called her

>A calliope programmed at the Lenin Institute.

After her visit to Hanoi in 1972, newspapers scoured Jane's background for juicy items to use. Her male friends from her Vassar days were most ungallant. 'Socially promiscuous.' 'So easy it was almost a joke.' Students in Los Angeles hanged a dummy of her after a mock treason trial. And in April 1973 Congressman Robert Steele, of Connecticut, said:

>I would like to nominate Jane Fonda for a special Oscar—for the rottenest, most miserable performance by an individual American in the history of our country.

From 1970, and her well publicized anti-Vietnam-war campaign, Jane became Public Enemy Number One to President Nixon and his right-hand man Henry Kissinger. Their paranoia about her grew to such lengths that she became the target for a virtual army of FBI, CIA and DIA surveillance men. Transcripts of her conversations went straight to the president. Her CIA file grew to 500 pages, many marked 'Grade I' and 'Top Secret'. She was down as a 'subversive' or 'anarchist'. One former agent confessed later: 'What Brezhnev and Jane Fonda said got about the same treatment.'

The Church Committee later revealed that FBI boss J. Edgar Hoover had personally authorized a government 'dirty tricks' unit in Los Angeles to try to discredit Jane with a planted item in a Hollywood gossip column. She was supposed to have gone to a fund-raising party for the Black Panther movement and called for the purchase of guns for the 'coming revolution'. And then, according to the story, she had led a refrain of 'We will kill President Nixon and any other mother-fuckers who get in our way'. It didn't sound very Jane Fonda.

Even her own father was sometimes against her. In 1971 he said:

>Sometimes when she talks to me her eyes widen almost like a madwoman and she screams about the injustices of American life. Listen to her on the telephone and she's like a fanatic.

Another famous name constantly on the receiving end recently is that of leggy Texan model Jerry Hall. Former beau Brian Ferry told how he was lucky to escape to marry heiress Lucy Helmore. 'Anyone who knows Jerry and knows my wife would realize how lucky I am being involved with a real person,' he said. And pop star Boy George, when collecting a pop award at London's Hilton hotel, made one of the cheapest and nastiest attacks on Ms Hall. 'What's the difference between the Eiffel Tower and Jerry Hall?' he asked. 'Easy. Not everyone has been up the Eiffel Tower.'

In the same league as the victim of cruel jibes is another famous girlfriend of the rock superstars, Britt Ekland. Even at home: once, when she washed her hair with a henna rinse, boyfriend Rod Stewart remarked, 'Mind someone doesn't mistake you for a carrot.'

But the most tasteless swipe at Britt came when she appeared on the British TV show *Punchlines*. Host Lennie Bennett read out the question: 'Who will give a tramp a bed for the night?' He added almost immediately: 'Britt Ekland?'

The producers had trouble persuading her to continue with the show.

One of the hallowed moments of American television came on the Johnny Carson show, with on-screen fisticuffs between Marlon Brando and Zsa Zsa Gabor. Brando had been warming up a little too heartily in the show's hospitality room and, by the time he appeared on screen, had consumed three bottles of champagne: he was spoiling for a fight. Midway through one of Zsa Zsa's spiels he turned to her and said: 'We going to listen to that crap all night?' Moment later the fighting started.

On the subject of fisticuffs, in February 1984 Hollywood legend Burt Lancaster went a little further than his tough-guy image should have let him when he set about his co-star, Margot Kidder, on the set of the film *Little Treasure*.

At first the film crew on Cuernavaca, Mexico, thought the vicious fight scene was a late addition to the script. But, as blood began to pour from Margot's mouth, executives had to separate the couple.

'I just don't know what came into me,' said 70-year-old Lancaster later.

Poor Cilla Black, appearing in pantomime in January 1985, was on the receiving end of a cruel comment from a young voice in the stalls. After she had asked the audience what they should do to get rid of King Rat, the biting reply came: 'Sing to him!'

Women can be so difficult to work with. The next project I work on I'd like to do with men only. I think I'd like to do a war film, somewhere where leading ladies don't exist. What bliss that would be.
Pierce Brosnan, 'Remington Steel' star, July 1984

6 You Must Be Joking

Brace yourself for a dip into the excruciating world of the worst sexist jokes—offered without comment (or my wife might hit me).

1st Demon: Ha, ha, ha!
2nd Demon: What's the joke?
1st Demon: I've just locked a woman in a room with 1,000 hats and no mirror.

A woman went to the doctors and said: 'I've got a pain in my leg.' The doctor said: 'It's old age.'

But the woman wasn't satisfied. 'I want a second opinion,' she demanded.

'OK,' said the doctor. 'You're ugly as well.'
Tommy Cooper

Definition of a truthful woman: a woman who doesn't lie about anything except her weight, her age, and her husband's salary.

'My girlfriend's 25 and has skin like a pearl.'
'She sounds beautiful.'
'Have you ever seen the skin of a 25-year-old pearl?'
Morecambe and Wise

My girlfriend was so skinny I took her to a restaurant and the waiter asked me to check my umbrella.
Mel Brooks

There was the dyed-in-the-wool cricket fan who got so absorbed in Test matches that he went to a psychiatrist.

'Doctor,' he blurted out, 'I've got cricket fever so badly I can't sleep any more. The minute I try to go off to sleep I see myself knocking Ian Botham for six, taking a catch in the slips off Joel Garner, or bowling to Alan Border.'

The psychiatrist had come across this problem before. Calmly he said, 'Our remedy has been effective for . . . if you'll pardon the expression . . . centuries.

'Just as you close your eyes, think of the most beautiful girl in the world and imagine you have her in your arms.'

'What!' said the cricket fan angrily. 'And miss my turn to bat?'

7 *Acid Repartee*

Thank God I won't have to act with you any more.
Katharine Hepburn to John Barrymore
I didn't know you ever had, darling.
John Barrymore to Katharine Hepburn

Some of the most vitriolic comments to women have been made in those most instantly memorable, always quotable, and often sparkling exchanges of biting repartee.

If you were my husband I'd poison your coffee.
Nancy Astor to Winston Churchill
If you were my wife, I'd drink it.
Winston Churchill to Nancy Astor

I've been a fan of Bob's since my mother took me to his first picture.
Lucille Ball on Bob Hope
I've known Lucy through five different shades of red hair.
Bob Hope on Lucille Ball

If you go on like that, I'll throw something at you.
Much harassed actress to Noël Coward

You might start with my cues.
Noël Coward to even more harassed actress

I hear you like them older these days.
Judy Carne to ex-husband Burt Reynolds after he took up with Dinah Shore, 19 years his senior
No, just classier.
Burt Reynolds to Judy Carne

Mr Churchill, I care neither for your politics nor your moustache.
Young female dining-companion to Winston Churchill
Don't distress yourself, you are not likely to come into contact with either.
Winston Churchill to young female dining-companion.

Didn't you write *Private Lives*? Not very funny.

> *Lady Diana Cooper, then starring in highbrow tragedy 'The Miracle', to Noël Coward*

Aren't you in *The Miracle*? Very funny indeed.

> *Noël Coward to Lady Diana Cooper*

Winston, you're drunk!

> *Bessie Braddock MP to Winston Churchill*

Bessie, you're ugly. And tomorrow morning I shall be sober.

> *Winston Churchill to Bessie Braddock*

I'm afraid I'm a little too tall for you, Mr Tracy.

> *Katharine Hepburn to Spencer Tracy*

Don't worry, he'll soon cut you down to size.

> *Joe Mankiewicz to both of them (the remark is usually wrongly attributed to Spencer Tracy)*

I'm sorry, I knew these lines backwards last night.

> *Struggling Claudette Colbert to Noël Coward*

And that's exactly the way you are saying them this morning.

> *Noël Coward to Claudette Colbert*

Finally: A revered, famous, but ageing movie star sat through the day's rushes, and then buttonholed the chief cameraman, Leon Shamroy. 'You are not,' she said, 'photographing my best side.'

'How can I?' he snapped. 'You're always sitting on it.'

DAMMIT THELMA, YOU DON'T EVEN LIKE <u>SINGLE</u> ENTENDRES

8 The Dirty Dozen: Twelve Top Male Chauvinists of Modern Times

Brooks, Lt.-Col. John Elliott, 'The Spanking Colonel'

Colonel Brooks, a London solicitor, former mayor and hunting squire, gained worldwide fame in 1974 in a sensational libel case that centred on his unusual hobby: spanking girls' bottoms. After he placed an advertisement in *Private Eye* for 'good-natured young ladies' to crew his yacht, the *Sunday People* investigated the 'duties' involved. The newspaper claimed that 'spanking squire' Brooks was 'a menace to young girls', and he sued for defamation. In court Brooks, a married man, was quite unabashed. Bottoms were made for beating, he said, and he had spanked 14 in all. The beatings were done with 'uninhibited candour', but always with the girls' consent.

The court exchanges had the nation on the edge of its . . . seat.

Mr Michael Eastham, QC: Do you get sexual pleasure by putting your hand up a woman's skirt when she is not wearing either tights or knickers?
Col. Brooks: Not sexual pleasure. Pleasure.

Mr Eastham on the girls on the boat: And you expected them to obey your every whim?
Col. Brooks: Yes. [He told the girls: 'I'm in command.']

All this was too much even for the judge, Mr Justice Bristow, who at one stage asked: 'Do you mean the girl had her whack?'

Brooks won the case but was awarded only a ha'penny damages, with each side having to pay their own costs. This was seen as a slap on the wrists, if not on the derrière, for the 'spanking colonel'.

Five years later, in June 1979, the *Sunday People* reported that Brooks was 'at it again'. He told a girl investigator that he was offering two weeks' training in being spanked, after which he hoped her bottom would graduate to a whip. Told he had been rumbled, Colonel Brooks invited his press tormentors to lunch at his club, telling them: 'Although my morals are disgusting, my manners are impeccable.'

Estrada, Eric

The Chips actor gets the vote for being just about the most beastly star to his wife. She alleged in her divorce deposition in September 1980 that he had forced her into sex and drug orgies, sent her a voodoo doll, tied her up, and threatened to shoot her (not necessarily in that order). And he had only been married seven months! Mrs Joyce Estrada, 40, told how he fired a gun into the bedroom ceiling and then told her the next bullet was for her. He said: 'I'm not the brash person everybody makes out.'

Hamilton, George

This actor and leading member of the Hollywood 'rat pack' has firm views on women: 'Count Dracula is really the ultimate in male chauvinist piggery. I think the Count and I have the same view on the ladies.'

'Gorgeous George' is a ladies' man, of course, and this is his example of how to treat them:

> I'm going out with four different girls—one for every mood. I've got one who's great at skiing and one who's marvellous with horses and another who likes to stay home and massage the back of my neck—they're hard to find, those. And if I want to go to a party there's always my ex-wife. Does that sound terribly selfish? Too bad.

Harris, Richard

Greatest of the hellraisers, this miller's son from Limerick does not appear to like women. 'I've had enough women in my life to know that lurking under that Helena Rubinstein exterior is a very vicious animal . . . [expletive deleted] insensitive savages, absolutely ruthless . . .'

> Marriage is a custom brought about by women who then proceed to live off men and destroy them, eating them away like a poisonous fungus on a tree.

He told his second wife, Ann Turkel: 'Gable and Lombard had fights and so should we.' Later: 'I've told her I don't want to hear her talking. If she agrees with something she can nod her head and if she doesn't she can shake it.' Surprise, surprise, not long afterwards the second Mrs Harris fled into the arms of Hans Bubringer, a burly and less chauvinistic Austrian.

Hughes Emlyn

The former Liverpool and England soccer captain, known to his friends as 'Crazy Horse' revealed on BBC TV's *A Question of Sport* in 1985 how he would win any chauvinist championship. His fantasy evening, he said, was lying on the settee watching football while his wife waited on him with fish and chips, before leaving her behind to join the lads at the local.

He told *The Sun* he was a chauvinist 'and proud of it'. 'I believe a woman's place is in the home and the man is boss,' he said. 'I do absolutely nothing in the house.' His favourite place he said, was a special corner of the pub 'where we stand and enjoy ourselves. We wouldn't want any woman around.'

Mr Hughes' lack of domesticity, said long-suffering wife Barbara, extended to thinking the microwave oven was a portable TV and trying to tune it to Channel 4. 'He doesn't know how to switch the cooker on. He'd starve if he were left at home. Once when I was at my mother's he rang up in a real paddy to ask me where the frozen chips were. I said "in the freezer" and he said "where's the freezer?"'

'The washing machine totally mystifies him. Once I'd gone to get a new fan belt for the Hoover. I rang Emlyn to check which size I wanted and he couldn't even open the cupboard, let alone get the vacuum cleaner out.'

McCririck, John

Known as 'Flash', the Old Harrovian ITV racing commentator gets the vote for an indiscreet interview with the *Daily Star* in March 1984 in which he had much to say. 'I married my wife because I fancied her dog. It was an ideal match for my labrador.' He added:

> I call my wife booby. That's the name of a South American bird which can't fly. It's so slow and stupid that it's always getting hit by planes on runways. But it's easy to catch. Booby suits my wife perfectly. She's SO dumb.

He informed the world that his wife's place was in the kitchen and she knew it:

> I never make a cup of tea, and wouldn't dream of touching the Hoover or doing housework. Men are women's Kings. To look after the man they have chosen, THAT's what makes them happy.

Women needed a firm hand, he said. Women's Lib was 'garbage'. It was when women believed they had rights that the real trouble began.

> Those Greenham Common women—there's nothing worse than a thinking woman. I'd drop a bomb on the lot of them.

Peppard, George

He stormed back to fame recently in *The A-Team* and was keen to prove he was top MCP on the set. He gladly admitted that he got actress Melinda Culea sacked from the show, and said he wanted to get her replacement, Marla Heasly, fired as well. 'I do not believe that *The A-Team* needs a woman in it,' he said. 'A woman tends to slow the whole thing down because she's only there for window-dressing. A woman is a distraction. Women are always silly in this kind of series.'

Reed, Oliver

If it came to naming the single greatest male chauvinist of the day, burly former stripclub bouncer Oliver Reed would be, to many, the automatic choice. When he arrived home one night in his Rolls Royce to find the MG car of his live-in love, Jacquie Daryl, in his way, he picked it up and flung it against a wall, causing several hundred pounds' worth of damage. Appearing on a TV chat show with Susan George, he suddenly made a grab for her; it ended up with the two of them in a writhingly suggestive heap on the studio floor. Said Susan:

> Oliver was just doing what he normally does. The only difference was that this was being televised live.

But, as a spokesman for the unseen millions of male chauvinists, Reed really has no equal.

The Thoughts of Chairman Ollie

- A woman's place is in the kitchen. It's security, where she can feed her children and her man.
- A woman should behave like a lady—like a nun in the kitchen by day and like a whore by night in bed. [Where have I heard this before?]
- It is the male who should choose the manner in which our society is determined. In no way should the dominance of the male be questioned.
- The woman on her knees in front of the man is not only exciting for the man; it should be extraordinarily successful for the woman.
- I tell them to 'shut up! I don't want to talk any more', and that's the end of it. And upon that my relationship with any woman is conducted. For conversation, I go to my local and talk to a lot of drunks.

I believe the greatest philosophies come out of the mouths of a few disillusioned men. But, sadly, most of them are like that because they are unhappy at the thought of being at home with their wives.
- I believe that women at the moment are making their men look like pansies and themselves like emancipated steam-hammers.
- Woman has blown her lib . . . these women are castrating men. I don't find it particularly attractive that these big bull dykes with flaccid knockers go screaming around talking about the liberation of the bra. Nobody is terribly interested in whether their knockers are in or out of the bra . . . These women have always been on the shelf.
- I'm still the sort of man who likes to go down to the pub on a Sunday and stand in one corner with the men. Women are so boring in pubs. All they talk about is washing-machines and nappies.

Almost the last word on Ollie came from a newspaper profile in 1982, after he had set up home with 17-year-old Josephine Burge. He was 'blissfully happy', said the writer. 'She pours his drinks, fills his pipe, and warms his slippers. She waits on his every whim . . . They later married.

Reynolds, Burt
Another Hollywood star who has a reputation of being mean with the opposite sex. Take this

interview in September, 1981:

> I'd like a woman who could be a classy, sophisticated lady and a total whore in bed. [There goes that phrase again.] She'd also have to be intelligent enough to know when to be quiet and·when to talk. She doesn't exist.

Nice guy.

Wales, HRH Charles, Prince of

With his old-fashioned shirts and ties and his unfashionable suits, Prince Charles seems permanently lingering two decades behind his peers. His biographer, Anthony Holden, painted a rather lurid picture of how the heir to the throne used to treat his lady friends:

> For at least one girl, an evening alone with the Prince meant listening to a long list of his conquests . . . he can also behave in a somewhat cavalier fashion; months can go by without a word, just when our heroine thought she had won a place in the Prince's heart.

On the requirements of a royal partner in those days, Holden said:

> . . . they call him 'Sir', even when alone with him. They will walk a pace or two behind him when protocol requires it. They know that, with few exceptions, it is he who issues the invitations, he who makes the phone calls . . . whatever the feelings of their heart, they are not allowed to forget the privilege his company bestows upon them.

Marriage does not seem to have altered the Prince. 'Marriage is all right but it interferes with my hunting,' he said soon after the wedding. Around the same time he pronounced:

> Although the whole attitude has changed towards what women are expected to do, I still feel, at the risk of sticking my neck out, that one of the most important roles any woman could ever perform is to be a mother.

Prince William arrived post-haste. Then, in June 1984, in St John's, Newfoundland, Charles spoke of plans for further children, saying: 'As parents, we realize the responsibility to our one child at present and I hope, several more in the future.' As he spoke, Diana lowered her head to hide her blushes, grimaced, and whispered: '*So* embarrassing.'

Wild, Judge David

He became a hate figure to thousands of women—and men—with a judgement in a rape case at Cambridge Crown Court in December 1982 in which a 35-year-old man was cleared. In his summing up, commonly described afterwards as a 'licence to rape', Judge Wild told jurors to remember the phrase 'stop it: I like it'. The woman raped said she hadn't screamed because of fright. Said Judge Wild:

> **It is not just a question of saying 'no'. It is a question of *how* she says it, how she shows it and makes it clear. If she doesn't want it, she only has to keep her legs shut and he would not get it without force. Then there would be marks of force being used.**

Cambridgeshire police destroyed the judge's case by saying: 'Our advice is that it is always better to submit to a rapist than face the prospect of violence.' Women Against Rape suggested his 'glib remarks' rendered him unfit to sit on a court bench.

Wolfe, Glynn 'Scottie'

In August, 1984, the man listed as 'the most married man in the monogamous world', Glynn H. 'Scottie' Wolfe, 75, of Blythe, California, was divorced again. He demanded a split from his 26th wife because

> I'm tired of women who don't want to stay home and wash clothes and do the ironing.

'Scottie', who first wed in 1927, had in fact made the same complaint about many of his previous wives—two of whom were women whom he had previously divorced. He reckoned being the Western World's most married man had cost him more than a million dollars in alimony over the years. Naturally, he had built up a vast stack of wedding albums and mementoes, including hundreds of pictures of his 40 children, which he kept under the much-used marriage-bed.

He said women were 'easy':

> I keep a bottle of whisky in the house. A large Scotch is the best pants-remover I know of.

9 Women: Troublesome Cattle

'Now women are mostly troublesome cattle to deal with mostly,'
said Goggins.
> Samuel Lover, eighteenth century

*M*en have been exaggerating women's shortcomings for centuries.

Woman the Nag
In February 1982 the *Daily Mail* unkindly reported that a German physiologist, a Dr Thiele, had made the 'startling discovery' that there is just one part of a woman's body which is superior to a man's . . . her tongue. 'The muscles are much stronger,' he reported.

> Generally speaking woman is generally speaking.
> *Anonymous*

Woman the Spendthrift
> Brigands demand your money or your life; woman requires both.
> *Samuel Butler*

> I only ever knew one woman who would not take gold—and she took diamonds.
> *Horace Walpole*

Woman the Fickle
> Fillies are like women—not to be relied upon. This is especially true early in the season.
> *'Daily Mirror Companion to Racing'*

> Woman is as false as a feather in the wind.
> *F. M. Piave, libretto for Verdi's 'Rigoletto'*

> A women's word is a bundle of water.
> *Hindu proverb*

Woman the Tyrant
> All wickedness is but little to the wickedness of a woman.
> *Ecclesiasticus 25:19*

> A wife is worse than a tennis coach—at least the coach goes home in the evening.
> *Ilie Nastase*

10 Nicknames

Rosalynn Carter was 'Evita'. To her male counterparts at Oxford, Shirley Williams will ever remain 'The Shetland Pony'. And who could think of Barbara Cartland as anything other than 'The Animated Meringue'?

One of man's instinctive ways of belittling a woman is to give her a nickname. Few are ever flattering. Most are callously abusive.

The successful adolescent star Tatum O'Neal has been variously 'Tantrum O'Neal', 'Little Miss Precocious' and 'Zsa Zsa'. And other 'pet names' have hardly been affectionate.

The she-wolf of France
> *Queen Isabella, wife of Edward II (he later had her murdered)*

Mrs Brown
> *Nickname for Queen Victoria after her infamous relationship with gillie John Brown*

Mrs Fagin
> *The Maharajah of Punjab's name for Queen Victoria (he resented her ownership of the Koh-i-Noor Diamond)*

Toothpick
> *Early nickname for the (then skinny) Sophia Loren*

The weeping widow
> *Mrs Sirimavo Bandaranaike, the world's first woman Prime Minister*

Beryl the Peril
> *US Under-Secretary for Monetary Affairs, Beryl Sprinkel*

Our Lady of Scowl
> *'Chicago Sun-Times' on Mayor Jane Byrne of the Windy City*

Worzel Gummidge
> *'Daily Mirror' nickname for Princess Anne because of her inelegant country clothes*

Our Val
> *Male members of the Royal Family on Princess Michael of Kent (short for 'valkyrie')*

When Esther Rantzen starred in one ill-fated show called *She and She* with Harriet Crawley, one male BBC wit christened the series 'Creepie and Crawley'. While left-wing MP Joan Maynard will always, to her male colleagues at least, be 'Stalin's Granny'.

The British satirical magazine *Private Eye* and its editor Richard Ingrams are specialists in assigning appalling and pornographic *noms de guerre*, and have come up with everything from the mildly eccentric 'Brenda' for the Queen and 'Yvonne' for Princess Margaret to, for battered wives campaigner Erin Pizzey, 'that vast pudding' and, most unkind of all, 'the lard mountain'.

But it's a rich field of male mischief.

SHOWBUSINESS

Burly Chassis	Shirley Bassey (by Terry Wogan)
Killer	Bo Derek (by her husband John)
Poopie	Britt Ekland (Rod Stewart's name for her)
The Queen Bitch of TV	Linda Gray (in her role as Sue Ellen in *Dallas*)
Leather Lungs	Elaine Paige
The Lofty Lefty	Vanessa Redgrave
Rusty Springboard	Dusty Springfield
No Neck	Charlene Tilton
The poison dwarf	Charlene Tilton

ALAS POOR DORIS

FIRST FAMILIES

The All-American Muppet	Amy Carter
The Steel Magnolia	Rosalynn Carter
Jackie O'Kinnock	Glenys Kinnock
Mama Kinnock	Glenys Kinnock
Porky Parry	Glenys Kinnock
The Queen	Nancy Reagan
Nancita	Nancy Reagan

HIGH SOCIETY

The Animated Meringue	Barbara Cartland (by Arthur Marshall)
Vindaloo	Edwina Currie, MP
The Bouncing Butter ball	Mrs Gwyneth Dunwoody, MP
The Ice Maiden	Chris Evert Lloyd
Miss Frigidaire	Chris Evert Lloyd
Miss Cool	Chris Evert Lloyd
Lady Forkbender	Marcia, Lady Falkender
Thunderthighs	Christina Onassis
The Greek Tanker	Christina Onassis
Whiplash	Anna Wallace

ROYALTY

Four-letter Annie	Princess Anne
Her Royal Haughtiness	Princess Anne
Her Royal Rudeness	Princess Anne
Princess Pea-brain	Princess Diana
The Champion O-level-getter of All Time	Princess Diana
Princess Pushy	Princess Michael of Kent
Rent-a-Royal	Princess Michael of Kent
BTL (= Billiard Table Legs)	Princess Michael of Kent
Miss Piggy	The Queen (after press secretary Michael Shea let it slip that the Royal Family call her severest public look her 'Miss Piggy Face')
Melons	Lady Helen Windsor (a reference to her well decorated chest)

MEDIA

Screech	Kate Adie, BBC TV News
The thinking man's crumpet	Joan Bakewell *and* Felicity Kendall
Jolly Sooper	Jilly Cooper
The Total Eclipse	Joanna Munro (a reference to her ample rear end)
Angela Cool	Angela Rippon
The Greek Pudding	Arianna Stassinopoulos
Arianna Bagwashinopoulos	Arianna Stassinopoulos

11 Favourite Targets for Male Bludgeons, Blunderbusses and Brickbats: The Royal Family

Her poisonous spittle could stop a camel in its tracks at 20 paces and blind a press photographer for life at twice the distance.
Auberon Waugh

. . . totally out of fashion and unique in her frumpiness.
Victor Fox, London fashion-store boss

It's tough being in the public eye, and with razor-sharpened sex-warrior tongues ready to slash forth, it's tougher still being a Royal, as Princess Anne has found out over the years to her cost. She didn't apply for the job—nor was she elected—but she does her best both for the British public and for international charities. It can't feel very uplifting, therefore, to be labelled:

This plain and pricey young woman
Willie Hamilton MP

Interminably obnoxious
Taki

The original pantomime dame
Auberon Waugh

The nub of it is she does not meet with male approbation as a 'glamorous bit of stuff' and she has suffered all over the world through male malice as a result. Naturally, in the end, she decided to have her own say. She told a gaggle of milling male photographers to 'naff off' and you might have expected that the press would have thought this way of non-swearing, without profanity or blasphemy, rather inventive.

Not a bit of it. Under the heading 'NAFF OFF ANNE—Your verdict on Her Royal Haughtiness,' the *Sunday People* in May 1983 ran an opinion poll which, it said, gave a 'brutally frank' message to her to go. People thought that the rest of the Royal Family would be better off without her.

Actually, only 43% of women questioned supported this view. So who was being 'brutally frank'? Yes, it was the young men of Britain, 59 per cent of whom wanted her into the Royal carriage and far, far away.

In August, 1975, the Italian magazine *Il Settimanale* called Anne 'One of the most boring people in the world today'—an award shared with Gina Lollobrigida, Golda Meir, Jackie Onassis and Margaret Thatcher.

In November 1978, John (perhaps surprisingly in the circumstances, later Sir John) Junor of the *Sunday Express* admonished her for refusing to cuddle a small boy during a tour of Norway. He wrote:

> Might it not be wise when she goes on goodwill tours abroad if instead of visiting sick children in hospitals she contents herself with administering sugar lumps in stables?

While in November 1982 Leslie Pine of *Burke's Peerage* wrote:

> What Queen Victoria would have thought of Princess Anne's language and public behaviour I shudder to think. For Her Royal Rudeness, as Anne is sometimes referred to, curses like a Billingsgate fish porter—if that is not an insult to Billingsgate fish porters.

Who else would put up with all this? An attempt was made to kidnap her in The Mall and barely anyone rushed to her aid. British Olympic athlete Daley Thompson, after winning his gold medal in Los Angeles, made tasteless cracks about 'making babies' with her. The *Washington Post* carried the cruel report that

> a man was found wandering in the grounds claiming he was in love with Princess Anne. He was later found to be mentally disturbed.

Even Prince Philip showed a most ungallant streak when he and his daughter were journeying together by plane. Philip went to see the flight deck and the pilot asked if Princess Anne would like to see the controls too. No, said the Prince:

> If it doesn't fart or eat hay she isn't interested.

*N*evertheless, Princess Anne isn't the only royal princess to find herself heavily on the receiving end. Viscount Linley said he would give his worst enemy a Christmas present of 'dinner with Princess Michael', while his mother, Princess Margaret, has been called:

> wayward . . . this expensive kept woman.
> *Willie Hamilton, MP*

> a parasite
> *Dennis Canavan, MP*

a royal baggage who has by her lifestyle forfeited all right to respect and homage
'Toronto Sun'

Said loudmouth MP Hamilton, long-time anti-monarchist narcissist:
> **She makes no attempt to conceal her expensive, extravagant irrelevance and it is impossible to make out any honest case of her being much use to anybody.**

*O*f course, she does not have to put up with quite the same as her sister, the Queen, who finds herself the target of every self-seeking publicity-grubbing male crackpot. Among unwelcome male attentions she has been the subject of:

The Sex Pistols They tried to cash in on publicity for the Silver Jubilee in 1977 with an offensive and obscene parody of 'God Save the Queen'.

King Hassan When she went on a state visit to Morocco in 1980 he tried to treat her like a fifth-class pizza waitress.

Tony Vermillion This Canadian designer, during her 1984 tour of North America, called her 'dowdy' and said that 'she seems to have stuck in the late 1960s'.

James Snow Ontario's Transport Minister and 'hick from the sticks' during the same trip kept touching her suggestively and holding her elbow.

Willie Hamilton Of course. He's called her 'a clockwork doll' and claimed she is 'mollycoddled to death'. There's too much more where that came from.

> If you feel you are to be presented to the Queen, do not rush up to her. She will eventually be brought round to you, like a dessert trolley at a good restaurant.
> *Advice in 'Los Angeles Times', 1983*

*T*he press has not always been kind. In 1972, after 20 years of the Queen's reign, the *News of the World* analyzed French press coverage of Britain's monarch. They found she had 'reliably' been said to have been

- **abdicating 63 times**
- **pregnant 92 times**
- **divorcing Prince Philip 112 times**
- **expelling Lord Snowdon from court 115 times**
- **rude to the Queen of Persia, Queen Fabiola of Belgium and Princess Grace of Belgium altogether 17 times**
- **rescued from assassination at the last minute 29 times**

France-Dimanche **has just carried an 'official' story that she had been forced to abdicate, claiming: 'A heavy sadness weighs on the British people . . .'**

The 'score', if anyone had chosen to try to add it up after 30 years, and in more countries than France, would surely have been virtually incalculable.

*E*ven our most favourite female Royals of today cannot, it seems, escape lashes of the male tongue. Taki has called Princess Diana 'as tough as an old boot', and Sunderland students once greeted her with a banner reading 'Hello Fertile Missie'. Willie Hamilton described her as 'a very lucky young woman with not many brains', while he said of that other favourite Queen Elizabeth the Queen Mother:

> The Royals all cultivate their image. And the Queen Mother—flashing that smile on and off—is the greatest gardener of the lot.

*A*nd, finally, the male-chauvinist quote to end all male-chauvinist quotes where royalty is concerned. In 1979, the Queen was on a tour of the remoter states of East Africa and was presented to one particularly obscure tribal chieftain.

Oh my God,
he was heard to splutter,
The Queen is a *woman*!

12 Top Mother-in-Law Jokes

Give up all hope of peace so long as your mother-in-law is alive.
Juvenal

Dragon, battleaxe, panzer unit—the mother-in-law is the favourite male resort for humour.

Every Christmas the wife's mother has been to our house for her dinner. This year we're having a change. We're going to let her in.
Les Dawson

Definition of mixed emotion: watching your mother-in-law drive off a cliff in your new car.

I invited a fellow round to my house the other night. Half way through the meal, he said: 'I don't like your mother-in-law.' So I said: 'That's all right. Leave her on the side of the plate and just eat the chips.'
Charlie Williams

She said to me: 'Don't you think I'd look terrific in something flowing.' I said 'Yes, try the River Thames.'
   Was she insulted?

I'll say. She went on and on about it. And did you give her as good as you got?
   Of course—I gave her a really good listening to.
Morecambe and Wise

Think you've got troubles? My mother-in-law has a twin sister.

I see in the paper that, in Germany, villagers have baked a giant omelette, 19 feet by 15 feet, weighing seven hundredweight.
   My mother-in-law baked an omelette that weighed seven hundredweight—and it was only five inches across.
Michael Aspel

A lawyer cabled one of his clients: 'Your mother-in-law passed away in her sleep last night. Shall we order burial, embalming, or cremation?'
   The client wired back: 'Take no chances. Order all three.'

13 The Critics

As antiseptic as an intensive care unit in a maternity hospital.
Clive James on Olivia Newton-John
Boiled down to the essentials, she is a plain mortal girl with large feet.
Herbert Kretzmer on Greta Garbo

Mean, vicious, venomous, cussed. One group of sex-warriors—and yes, they invariably *are* men—forms the insult-hurling elite. These are the people who get paid for the poison.

Stars of the Small Screen

A neckless blonde sex grenade only half as high as anyone else.
Clive James on Charlene Tilton

Looking like a strawberry lolly with a voice like a broody hen, she is a disaster.
Simon Kinnersley, 'The Sun', on Cilla Black in 'Surprise, Surprise!'

She tackles a role as if it were a sirloin and she doesn't care who was looking.
James Agee on Lucille Ball

The Divine Miss Midler

She sings, not too well, but very loudly and recklessly, for all the world like a delirious female impersonator.
David Robinson, 'The Times'

Miss Midler is what America now has instead of a three-ring circus.
Sheridan Morley

She offers the audience about as much in the way of charm as Heinrich Himmler.
David Robinson, 'The Times'

Her voice is all it's cracked up to be: it lacks range, accuracy, and control.
Bart Mills, 'Daily Mail'

The Misunderstood Miss Minnelli

I always thought Miss Minnelli's face deserving of first place in the Beagle category. It is a face always going in three directions simultaneously. The nose en route to becoming a trunk, blubber lips unable to resist the pull of gravity, and a chin trying its damnedest to withdraw into the neck, apparently to avoid responsibility for what goes above it.

John Simon, 'New York' magazine

The Indelible Miss Taylor

When she plays Cleopatra as a powerful animal, she screeches like a ward heeler's wife at a block party.

'Time'

She is fat and will do nothing about her most glaring defect, an unpleasant voice which she cannot adequately control.

'Life' on 'Boom!'

When she welcomes Burton [playing Faustus] to an eternity of damnation her eyeballs and teeth are dripping pink in what seems to be a hellish combination of conjunctivitis and trench mouth.

'Time' on 'Dr Faustus'

At 45, Elizabeth Taylor reminds one of the trademark for Mike Todd's *Around the World in 80 Days*—one hot-air balloon.

'Esquire'

TV Presenters, Anchorwomen and Newsreaders

She presented the Booker Prizes with all the easy aplomb of a prop forward on valium.

Charles Nevin, 'Sunday Telegraph', on Selina Scott

. . . as awful as ever. With her flashing teeth and frightening smile, she looks more and more like one of Dr Who's opponents, the Queen of Planet Beeb, perhaps.

Richard Ingrams on Esther Rantzen

Her comic music-hall accent was amusing for the first minute or so but combined with her arrant amateurishness in a serious interview it became farcical.

Richard Afton, 'Evening News', on Arianna Stassinopoulos

She is reputed to earn more money than any other woman in Fleet Street, for reasons which escape me. Probably she draws the bulk of her massive screw in danger money, to offset the lacerating cortical damage she must sustain when reading her own prose.

Clive James on Jean Rook

Her face has more character than the other female newsreaders, mainly because of the wrinkles.

> *Chris Greenwood, 'Sunday'*
> *magazine, on Sarah Hogg*

Fright sight of the week . . . she looked as though someone had poured a pot of red paint over her head.

> *Charles Catchpole, 'The Sun', on*
> *TV newsgirl Linda Lewis*

Singing in Vain

Looking about as innocent as Hitler, and twice as ambitious.

> *Stafford Hildred, 'Daily Star', on*
> *Sheena Easton*

Looking like a vulgar Christmas tree, all glitter and no naturalness, she sang a song and deepened the mystery of how she ever became a pop star.

> *Richard Afton on Patti Boulaye*

She looked like one of the chorus girls in *The Muppets*. Her voice will do wonders for the sale of earplugs.

> *'The Sun' on Sarah Brightman*

Modern Critical Classics

And if they're not already, they deserve to be:
So sweet she could give you tooth decay at 50 paces.

> *Anonymous critic on Julie Andrews*

All pouting surface unsupported by talent.

> *Tom Hutchinson on Pia Zadora*

Sizzles like a wet banana.

> *Ivan Waterman, 'News of the*
> *World', on Bo Derek in 'Bolero'*

While Pamela Stephenson may look as fresh as a dairymaid, she also sings like a dairymaid who has stood in something even fresher.

> *Jack Tinker*

A performance so wooden, she ought to be investigated for dry rot.

> *Anonymous critic on Fiona*
> *Richmond*

14 Grounds for Divorce

The man who marries always makes the woman a present
because she needs marriage and he does not . . . Woman is
made for man, man is made for life.
Henri de Montherlant, 'Young Girls'

Nowhere, perhaps is *Homo chauviens* more devastatingly revealed than in the divorce courts. Every week the papers are full of 'mental cruelty' cases showing at least that man hasn't lost his powers of invention when it comes to keeping the fair sex down . . .

A young bride called Ilse blushed with pride when her husband Paul gave her 10 out of 10 for her first lovemaking session, and 10 out of 10 for her first dinner. But then his compulsion for arithmetic started to get her down.

Each week, a divorce court in Munich heard, he insisted on marking her for: behaviour during the week; cooking; cleanliness; attitude to other men; and accomplishments in bed.

'Paul behaved like a pedantic schoolmaster, always carping and fault-finding,' she said. 'Each week he examined my housekeeping book searching for errors.'

The final straw came, the court heard, one night after Paul gave Ilse 2 out of 10 for performance and 0 out of 10 for effort.

She went home to mother.

American stuntman George Sawaya offered to swap his wife for a new car, Jean Olsen, 24, sobbed as she told a divorce judge in Los Angeles:

> We met a man we didn't even know who had a new car which George admired. The man told George he was the luckier of the two because George had a pretty wife.
>
> That's when George offered to swap me for this car. He told the man he would rather have a new car than a wife because he could turn in a car for a new one—but couldn't turn in a wife for a new model.

Jean got her divorce, plus maintenance to support her three-year-old son.

Mrs Nora Dady, 36, of Poplar, was granted a divorce in London on the grounds of her husband's smelly feet. She said guillotine-operator Cornelius Dady, 55, wouldn't wash regularly, had only one bath a week, and wouldn't change.

'A deadly atmosphere built up in the matrimonial home,' the court was told.

Irmgard Prien of Hanover obtained a divorce in 1978 after complaining of her husband's collection of 232 cuckoo clocks. She had endured the chiming, buzzing and cuckooing for three years, but had finally said enough was enough. She was awarded custody of the matrimonial home . . . minus the clocks.

The local cricket club were named by Mrs Mildred Rowley as 'the other woman' at a divorce hearing in Wolverhampton. She said her 48-year-old husband Mike 'obsession' with bat and ball was 'bordering on madness'. The court heard how he had moved out of the family home and into the cricket pavilion owned by Stourbridge Town, to camp out among the pads and bats. 'He could tell you who scored what years ago, but he never remembered my birthday,' she said on being awarded a divorce for her husband's unreasonable behaviour.

Mike Rowley did not contest the action, and in any event was unable to attend the hearing because he was on tour with his team in Devon. Contacted at a cricket ground at Torquay, he said: 'Cricket always came first with me. I wouldn't go to my daughter's confirmation or my granddaughter's christening. That caused trouble—they clashed with cricket. Though I did go to my mother-in-law's funeral.' Brushing past reporters he added: 'There's nothing more that I can say. I cannot stop . . . we have to get on with the game . . .'

Joseph Ernst, 46, had a novel suggestion when he returned from a nine-month stint working as a civil engineer in Bangkok. He told his wife Marita, 36, that he expected her to behave like 'those dusky, almond-eyed Thai beauties'. In other words, he wanted her to be his sex slave.

Marita, of Rheinbach, near Bonn, applied for a divorce in 1973 after she told how she was expected to bow before him, touching the floor with her forehead, as a sign of obedience. She then had to anoint his body with fragrant and expensive Oriental oils. He told her to kiss his feet before lovemaking 'to show total submission like the girls do in Thailand'.

But the final straw, she said, came when she scalded a sensitive spot during the ceremony of kneeling, bare-bosomed tea-serving.

Tightwad Bill Broadhurst was branded 'Mr Mean' and 'Britain's meanest husband' in a 1983 divorce case. The London High Court Family Division heard that during 36 years of marriage to 56 year-old Thelma he had devised a scale of penny-pinching charges:

FOR driving Thelma to work during a rainstorm . . . the cost of the petrol
FOR decorating the living-room ceiling . . . £5 an hour

FOR electricity used by the family when they watched television . . . 50p a week
FOR the hot water used by his daughter when she popped round for a shower . . . 5p

Mr Justice Eastham said that bricklayer Bill was 'a very selfish, insensitive man' who was interested only in playing golf and bowls. He never bought Thelma a birthday present, and he refused to contribute to the cost of the wedding when his daughter married.

Mr Broadhurst said: 'It is true I charged the family for electricity used by the TV. But that was because my only joy was to listen to the radio, and they froze me out of the front room. The family ganged up on me. I was the henpecked worm in the house.

Thelma, granted a divorce, agreed that he wasn't as mean as the judge had portrayed him. 'He was even worse.'

In a case that made French legal history, a woman from Dieppe was granted a divorce from her 70-year-old barber husband after complaining that he could not stop chasing her round the house demanding sex. The court heard that Ishmael Franconville-Moulter—the

'demon barber'—a great-grandfather, was so highly-sexed that he chased his wife relentlessly, hitching up her skirt and covering her with kisses.

She said it was 'against nature' and that he was 'a demon'.

The (female) judge, Maria-Thérèse Chesnelang, agreed, and said that a man aged 70 who 'devoured his wife' by demanding relationships of an 'unnatural' kind was 'abusing his rights in a way likely to cause serious injury to a woman of similar age'.

Mme Franconville-Moulter was granted a divorce on the grounds of the demon barber's 'excessive virility'.

Seven-stone Pamela Aihie, 49, of Hornchurch, Essex, was granted a divorce in March 1985 after a judge heard how her bad-tempered doctor husband used to pin her in a corner if she disagreed with him. He weighed 18 stone—and would stand on her toes until she agreed with him. 'This marriage clearly got off to a bad start,' said Mr Justice Reeve.

Ursula Torday, 55, of Vienna, was awarded a divorce because her husband filled their flat with his vast collection of beermats. She complained of a lost sex-life and said: 'Because of the beermats, there was hardly any room to turn round in bed.'

And finally . . . When Americans Virgil Everhart and his wife Janice decided to part after 20 years of marriage they had a problem about splitting everything down the middle. She drove off in the family car with the two children, and sent him a legal letter demanding that he pay her rent, housekeeping, utilities and a weekly sum.

Virgil bitterly decided to take his own action. 'She has my car and more than half my money. I decided to divide the property before she got that as well.'

So he got hold of a chain-saw and started splitting their home . . . right down the middle. He started by cutting a six-inch gap in the floor of their 30ft by 35ft timber house, and within 24 hours had ruined three chains tearing through nails and wiring.

He said: 'I've picked my half—the living room and one bedroom. She can have the kitchen and one bedroom.' The bathroom was a problem, but Virgil compromised by cutting it clean in half—including the bathtub, which he sliced in two with a blowtorch.

County circuit court clerk Jo Peveler drove out to see Virgil at work, and reported: 'It's a pretty neat job, as far as it goes. They only have one dog, though, and he was looking pretty worried when I left.'

15 Woman: Body, Heart, Mind and Soul

This unfortunate anatomy, which seems wanting in significance by itself.
Jean-Paul Sartre

Body

The female body, even at its best, is very defective in form; it has harsh curves and very clumsily distributed masses; compared to it the average milkjug, or even cuspidor, is a thing of intelligent or gratifying design . . . below the neck by the bow and below the waist astern there are two masses that simply refuse to fit into a balanced composition. Viewed from the side, a woman presents an exaggerated 'S' bisected by an imperfect straight line, and so she inevitably suggests a drunken dollar-mark.
H. L. Mencken

Heart

Women's hearts are like old china, none the worse for a break or two.
W. Somerset Maugham

Mind

Women's intuition is the result of millions of years of not thinking.
Rupert Hughes

In a certain sense their brains are in their wombs.
Havelock Ellis, pioneer sexologist

What harm can her foolishness do to a woman?
Charles Baudelaire (1821–1867)

Soul

A woman mov'd is like a fountain troubled,
Muddy, ill-seeming, thick, bereft of beauty.
William Shakespeare, 'The Taming of the Shrew'

Despite my thirty years of research into the feminine soul, I have not yet been able to answer . . . the great question that has never been answered: *What does a woman want?*
Sigmund Freud

16 King Bitch

She looks like a flower child who went to seed in a cabbage patch
On Barbra Streisand

Like two small boys fighting under a mink blanket
On Elizabeth Taylor

She reminds me of the elephant in *Dumbo* with all its glittering trappings
On Zsa Zsa Gabor

*W*ithout doubt he's THE champion insult-hurler of all time. Impish Hollywood couturier Richard Blackwell began his 'worst-dressed list' in 1960 after a failed career as an actor and a dancer, and it has brought him more fame than any of his clothes ever did. He says his victims should be thankful to him: 'Where are they going to get that much publicity unless they murder their mothers?

So, brace yourselves for the best insults of 25 years from the king bitch, Mr Blackwell.

Princess Anne
The Royal automechanic . . . Her costumes are hippie jokes . . . She even makes the Queen look fashionable and that takes some doing.

Lucille Ball
Her motto must be, if you can't wear it, carry it.

Brigitte Bardot
A buxom milkmaid wearing a girdle.

Pamela Bellwood (of *Dynasty*)
She resembles the living end of the endangered species.

Cher
Setting femininity back 20 years.

Joan Collins
Fighting it out for the tacky-taste crown of the Forties.

Patti Davis (daughter of Ronald Reagan)
Packs all the glamour of an old, worn-out sneaker.

Princess Diana
> A nightmare . . . It looks as if Shy Di has invaded Queen Victoria's attic . . . Like a Mack Sennet bathing beauty . . . Dusty and frumpy-looking—she is turning into a carbon-copy of the Queen.

Angie Dickinson
> Venus covered in a fishnet.

Mia Farrow
> With that haircut she should go into a monastery. No, I didn't say a convent, I said a monastery.

Judy Garland
> Poor thing—apparently she left all her fashionable clothes in that trunk she is always singing about.

Goldie Hawn
> A shaggy dog on stilts wearing a band-aid.

Queen Juliana of the Netherlands
> All the Queen's horses and all the Queen's men, couldn't make Juliana look good again.

Nancy Kissinger
> A travelling fashion stew.

Louise Latter (actress)
> This summer's tumbleweed.

Cyndi Lauper
> Looks like the aftermath of the San Francisco earthquake.

Shirley Maclaine
> She looks as if everyone she knows has given her something to wear.

Princess Margaret
> To catalogue her sartorial shortcomings would require a whole column to take her apart, and she needs it . . . She killed the midi just by wearing it.

Bette Midler
> Pot luck in a laundromat . . . Second-hand Rose after the hurricane.

Jackie Onassis
> Her wedding-dress was a disgrace—she did everything to make herself look 17, which I thought was very rude when she was marrying someone twice her age.

The Queen
> What she wore for President Ford's banquet looked like Ali McGraw had crotcheted her this hat and it had shrunk on the way to New York.

Brooke Shields
> She looks like a Halloween trick without the treat.

Charlene Tilton
> A Victorian lampshade holding her breasts.

Sharlene Wells (Miss America)
> She looks more like an armadillo with corn-pads.

17 Favourite Targets for Male Bludgeons, Blunderbusses and Brickbats: Margaret Thatcher

I wouldn't say she was open-minded on the Middle East, so much as empty-headed. She probably thinks Sinai is the plural of Sinus.
Jonathan Aitken, MP

In terms of achievement by merit, Margaret Hilda Thatcher has become one of the most successful women in history. For precisely this reason she has also been one of the most vilified and abused members of the female sex since Joan of Arc.

Uniquely snubbed by male dons at Oxford in 1985, she has been compared unfavourably with Hitler, Attila, Mussolini, Pétain, Marie Antoinette, witches, dragons, dinosaurs . . . **And the meanest insults have all come from men.**

Even her close colleague and deputy Willie Whitelaw confided: 'I found her, well . . . rather frightening.'

WHAT WOULD *YOUR* LIFE BE LIKE UNDER MRS THATCHER'S BROOMSTICK?
Headline in 'Daily Mirror'

A dictator bound by her own personal prejudices.
Neil Kinnock

Maggie Thatcher is the worst thing that's happened to this country since the Black Death.
John Livingstone, secretary of Liverpool's Vauxhall ward Labour Party

During the run-up to the Falklands crisis US Secretary of State Alexander Haig took part in frantic negotiations with the Argentines.
Finally, on leaving Buenos Aires, he told them:
You don't know that lady but I do. She is frightening. God help you.

And during the UN Security Council debate on the Falklands, Panama's foreign minister attributed to Mrs Thatcher's tough stance on the South Atlantic to 'the glandular system of women'.

> Margaret Thatcher is doing for monetarism what the Boston Strangler did for door-to-door salesmen.
> *Denis Healey*

> Sir—Brian Walden was inaccurate to liken Mrs Thatcher to Franklin Roosevelt. Franklin Roosevelt created jobs, Mrs Thatcher destroys them. It is difficult to find any historical parallel to Mrs Thatcher—except for hard-hearted Hannah, the girl from Savannah, famous for throwing water on a drowning man.
> *Letter in 'London Evening Standard'*

*U*S information-service director Charles Wick had to apologize in December 1983 for 'making a sexist remark' when he told a group of Californian editors: 'Mrs Thatcher opposed the US invasion of Grenada because she is a woman.' After his audience groaned, he pleaded: 'Please don't print what I said. I'll never get back to London.'
They printed it.

*S*imon Hoggart has told how one Conservative minister used to be prone to walking around Westminster using 'Thatcher' as a substitute for a slightly less agreeable word. He would say 'Thatcher me!'; 'I've had an absolute Thatcher of a day' and 'I'm absolutely Thatchered'. Hoggart is coy about who the minister was and whether he was ever promoted; if not, you can assume he feels 'a bit of a silly Thatcher' now.

*O*ne senior Conservative who clearly does not like Mrs Thatcher's style is former premier Harold Macmillan, now Lord Stockton. Asked in 1984 what his future plans were, he said: 'I would very much like to go to Margaret Thatcher's funeral.'
Meeting former British premiers Heath and Callaghan at a dinner (and indirectly referring to the Lords Home and Wilson) he said: 'There are so many ex-Prime Ministers alive right now, we could form a club.' As Heath and Callaghan nodded their approval he added: 'And we wouldn't have any women in it, would we?'
In 1983, outside his home at Highgrove, a relative helped him into the awaiting car. 'Ah, I see we're going in a Thatcher!' he declared. Why was that, asked the relative. 'Well,' said the mischievous Supermac, 'when the doors open, lights come on. When you don't fasten your belt it makes a terrible noise at you. It's a *bossy* sort of car.'

She talks to people as if they were three.
Norman St John Stevas

She doesn't even know how to *spell* the word 'negotiate'.
Francis Pym

When Labour left-winger Dennis Canavan called Mrs Thatcher, during Scottish question time, 'That demented woman!', he was admonished by the Speaker of the House of Commons for using quite unparliamentary language.

'I withdraw, Mr Speaker,' Canavan said. 'I meant the Right Honourable demented woman.'

And an item on ITV's breakfast channel, TV-am, produced the following exchange:

Paul Johnson: Mrs Thatcher is what I'd call a handbag economist.
Neil Kinnock: You mean, 'if you don't stand in line I'll hit you with my handbag.'

A favourite game played by Mrs Thatcher's more disloyal colleagues was to ask: if she were run down by a No. 11 bus tomorrow, who would you pick as your leader? When they were still very firmly attached to Mrs Thatcher's rival Edward Heath, the Young Conservatives carried out a poll on the subject. The voting was: Edward Heath, 20 per cent; Jim Prior, 12 per cent; Lord Carrington, 10 per cent; and so on. The winner, however, with a thumping 49 per cent, was 'the driver of the bus'.

'Santa' Charlie Chatburn was not very merry in his grotto at Debenham's, Manchester, in November 1985 when three-year-old Matthew Delaney sat on his knee and asked for a water pistol for Christmas. In fact, Mr Chatburn was rather gung-yo-ho-ho.

'You should get a real gun and shoot Mrs Thatcher,' was the Father Christmas's festive quip.

She looked like a starlet auditioning for a bit part in *Dracula*.
Chris Buckland, 'Sunday People', on her Dutch TV appearance

She sounds like a bloody Martian—completely out of touch with the human world.
Retired postal union chief Tom Jackson

I reckon she was Anne Boleyn in a previous life—all charm and no head.
Retired civil-service union chief Ken Thomas

If I were married to her, I'd be sure to have dinner ready when she got home.
George Shultz

She has much in common with the Thatcher pound coin—it's thick, brassy, and thinks it's a sovereign.
Neil Kinnock

Thatcher jokes abound, and it is perhaps wise to restrict ourselves to the three very worst. Broadcaster Terry Wogan is just one of many who have told how Mrs Thatcher's husband Denis had passed away, and a friend enquired: 'Did he speak any last words.'

'No,' he was told. 'She was with him till the end.'

She was asking to be buried on a certain spot in the Holy Land. The Israeli Government says, 'It'll cost you £2 million,' and she replies: 'That's a bit much for three days.'
Bernard Manning

When Britain was an Empire we were ruled by an Emperor. When we were a kingdom we were ruled by a king. And now we're a country we're ruled by Margaret Thatcher.
Kenny Everett

87 NASTY NAMES FOR MRS T
Fined £50 for throwing a rotten egg at Mrs Thatcher during a visit to Milton Keynes in 1985, jobless teenager Paul Sykes said: 'I meant to get the old boot.'

As Britain's most successful post-war Premier she deserves none of this. But because she's a woman and has offended the male psyche she has been heavily on the receiving end. Just consider the name-calling:
Arthur Daley—*Norman Willis*
Attila the Hen from Number 10—*Arthur Scargill*
Bambi with missiles
Bargain-Basement Boadicea—*Denis Healey*
The Beached Shark—*Alan Watkins*
Big Sister—*Dr David Owen*
The Bitch
The Blessed Margaret—*Norman St John Stevas*
Mrs Blue Rinse
La Bombolla (the doll)—*President Craxi of Italy*
The Boss—*Private Eye*
The Bossette—*Lord Carrington*
Miss Bossy
Bossy Boots
Calamity Jane—*Denis Healey*
Catherine the Great of Finchley—*Denis Healey*
The Cold War Bitch
The Cold War Warrior—*Roy Mason*
The Cuckoo of British Politics—*David Steel*
David Owen in Drag—*Rhodesia Herald*
Diamond Lil—*The Sun (on South Africa)*
Dictator—*Neil Kinnock*
Dolly Parton—*Julian Barnes*
The Dragon Empress—*Denis Healey*
An Egotistical Flea in a Fit—*Neil Kinnock*
The Enemy Abroad—*Gerald Kaufman*
Evita

Mrs Finchley—*from a slip of the tongue by David Dimbleby*
The Fishwife—*Gerald Kaufman*
Miss Floggie—*Denis Healey*
The Gesticulating Pygmy—*Gerald Kaufman*
Glenda Jackson—*Paul Callan*
Gloriana
The Goddess of War and Want—*John Pilger*
The Great She-Elephant—*Denis Healey*
The Grocer's Daughter—*Private Eye*
Hard-hearted Hannah
The Headmistress
Heather
Hilda
Miss Iceberg—*Daily Star*
The Immaculate Misconception—*Norman St John Stevas*
The Iron Lady—*Red Star (Moscow)*
The Iron Maiden
Jezebel—*Rev Ian Paisley*
Lady Falklander
Lady Macbeth—*Roy Hattersley*
The Leaderene—*Norman St John Stevas*
Marie Antoinette—*Peter Shore*
The Mad Thatch
Mark Thatcher's minder
The Most Hated Prime Minister—*Tony Benn*
Mother—*Tory backbenchers*
Much hairdo about nothing
Mrs Mugabe
Old Mrs T—*Joe Ashton*
One Woman Task Force
The Original Cabbage Patch doll
The Parrot—*Edward Heath*

La Pasionaria of Middle-Class Privilege—*Denis Healey*
The Patron Saint of Milliners
Patron Saint of the rich
Pétain in Petticoats—*Denis Healey*
Phantom of the Westminster Opera
The Plutonium Blonde—*Arthur Scargill*
The Poujadiste—*Michael Heseltine, quoted by the Guardian*
The Queen of Monetarism
The Queen of Sheba—*Lord Stockton*
Rambona—*Denis Healey*
The Reluctant Debutante
Rhoda the Rhino—*Denis Healey*
She Who Must Be Obeyed
Snobby Roberts—*school nickname*
Stupid Woman—*Eric Heffer*
Madame Suharto—*Dennis Skinner*
TBW (That Bloody Woman)—*Dennis Canavan*
Thatcher Milk-snatcher
That Demented Woman—*Dennis Canavan*
Tina ('There Is No Alternative')
Twister—*Neil Kinnock*
The Uranium Lady—*French newspaper*
A walking ad for hair laquer
The Westminster Ripper—*Dennis Skinner*
Winston Churchill in drag—*Denis Healey*
The Witch of Finchley
The Wolverine

18 More Top Sexist Jokes

Trouble and Strife

The wealthy businessman returned home early one day quite unexpectedly and found his wife in the arms of his best friend. He looked at his friend disdainfully and said: 'Dick, I must. But you?'

The chemist met his old friend on the golf course and asked: 'Well Tom, did that mudpack I recommended improve your wife's looks?'

    'It did for the first two weeks,' said Tom mournfully, 'but then it wore off.'

She was standing on the beach when a policeman came along. He said: 'Excuse me madam, you'll have to move. The tide wants to come in.'

I wouldn't say she was mean, but they made 50p pieces that shape so they could get them out of her hand with a spanner.

In a darkened cemetery, a grief-stricken man stood stooping over a grave for seven days running. Disconsolately beating his breast, he kept sighing mournfully, 'Oh, why did he have to die, why did he have to die?'

A gravedigger sought to console him and said: 'Was it your father? Or your brother, maybe?'

    'No,' sobbed the mourner. 'He was my wife's first husband.'

Give a Woman an Inch and She'll Park in it

'I turned the way I signalled,' she said indignantly after the smash.

    'I know,' said the man she'd hit. 'That's what fooled me.'

A woman motorist was sauntering along a country lane when she noticed two linemen climbing telegraph poles. 'Cowards,' she muttered to her companion. 'They must think I've never driven a car before.'

The examiner was testing a male applicant for a driving licence. 'What does it mean,' he asked, 'when a woman is holding out her hand?'

    'Well,' replied the young hopeful. 'You can be sure that she is turning left, turning right, backing up, doing a three-point turn, waving at somebody, or going to stop.'

19 Classic Vitriol

Working with her is like being hit over the head with a Valentine's card.
Christopher Plummer on Julie Andrews after 'The Sound of Music'

*W*hen it comes to man at his most acid, sex-war oldies are goodies, and prince of the put-down was undoubtedly American critic-turned-playwright George S. Kaufman. It was he who told flour-heir's wife Ruth Fleischmann:

> You're a birdbrain, and I mean that as an insult to birds.

But perhaps the most devastating riposte was to Ruth Gordon, who described a new play to him:

> There's no scenery at all. In the first scene, I'm on the left side of the stage and the audience has to imagine I'm in a crowded restaurant. In Scene Two, I run over to the right side of the stage and the audience has to imagine I'm home in my own drawing-room.

'And the second night,' said Kaufman, '*you*'ll have to imagine there's an audience out front.'

*S*ome of the great male put-downs go back a little further into history. Scorned philosopher Friedrich Nietzsche waxed lyrical on his one-time lover Lou Andreas-Salome, calling her inventively:

> That scraggy dirty she-monkey with false breasts.

But then Nietzsche's views on women in general were idiosyncratic:

> When a woman becomes a scholar there is usually something wrong with her sex organs.

Competing with Nietzsche in the rudery stakes was the French statesman, Georges Clemenceau. He had a ready response when challenged while sitting in his carriage by a woman of no uncertain bulk. 'Oh, monsieur,' she told him. 'I suffer from wind something awful.'

'Then fart, my good woman, fart!' he replied.

*S*ome more classic vitriol . . .

Julie Andrews

A hideous child with pigtails, corked teeth and very bad legs.
Val Parnell

Lauren Bacall

A middle-aged woman trying to hang onto her glamour.
Tony Curtis

Lucille Ball

The voice is like rough gravel. The face is a map of a hundred journeys—all of them ending at the bank.
Anonymous male critic

Rosalynn Carter

She works at being First Lady like a programmed robot.
'Daily Express'

Bette Davis

I can't imagine any guy giving her a tumble.
Carl Laemmle

Doris Day

I knew her before she was a virgin.
Oscar Levant

Britt Ekland

She's gone to the Virgin Islands to be recycled.
Bob Monkhouse

Marcia, Lady Falkender

By the time Harold Wilson went out of Downing Street in April 1976 there were only two views about her being held by her staff, and they are both unprintable.
Joe Haines

The secret of Marcia Williams' remarkable success is her extraordinary talent for being overrated.
Roy Hattersley

Jean Harlow

The only person I know shaped like a dustpan.
Joseph March, screenwriter

Vivien Leigh

You sound like someone's got their finger up your ass.
George Cukor on her screen-test for 'Gone With The Wind'

Golda Meir

She fits all the Jewish jokes. As a mother and grandmother she is unmistakeably the kind of lady Portnoy complained about.
John Akass, 'Sun'

Marilyn Monroe

Directing her was like directing Lassie.
Otto Preminger
Like kissing Hitler.
Tony Curtis, on playing love-scenes with her

Margaret O'Brien

If that child had been born in the Middle Ages she'd have been burned as a witch.
Lionel Barrymore

Yoko Ono

Preposterous . . . a foreshortened and mildly ga-ga Geisha girl.
Donald Zec, 'Daily Mirror'
What she had was no secret to anyone. Always walking round the kitchen undressed she was. And it wasn't a pretty sight.
Leslie Anthony, chauffeur to the Beatles

Tessie O'Shea

She doesn't have a bath, she goes to the car-wash.
Bernard Manning

Elizabeth Taylor

Who needs her? Any hundred-dollar-a-week girl can play Cleopatra.
Joe Moskowitz, vice-president of Fox

Something ghastly has happened over the course of her last four or five films. She has become a hideous parody of herself—a fat, sloppy, yelling screeching banshee . . .
Rex Reed

20 It's Still a Male, Male World

I've got a reputation for being a male chauvinist pig, you know.
But when women throw themselves at you all the time,
sometimes the only way to treat them is—badly. And when you
do that, you get a bad reputation.
Jack Nicholson

A doctor jilted by a local girl in Susanville, California, decided to get his own back on women—by turning his mansion home into a 'house of horrors'. Dr Edwin Sandy spent $150,000 on his 'dream', then invited the prettiest girls in the neighbourhood to 'housewarmings'—where their degradation could be watched by fellow male chauvinists.

- High-pressure airjets were turned on, blowing their skirts and dresses above their heads.
- As one woman elegantly descended the stairs, they flattened out, propelling her into a group of hooting, mocking males.
- Women who used cosmetics put out for them in the ladies' room found that the face-powder turned their faces green and that the lipstick went black.
- After tea women were encouraged to lie down upstairs. On the bedroom ceilings they saw paintings of historical scenes where women had 'betrayed' men. Settling on the bed activated mournful tape recordings of Dr Sandy telling of the menace of faithless womankind.
- One girl screamed as she found her bed suddenly hurtling towards a brick wall. At the last minute the wall opened and she fell headlong into a room full of laughing men.
- Other girls took a dip in the pool. They clambered out distraught—in the water there was an alligator.

Local girls soon got wise to Sandy's 'parties'. But he continued his sadistic 'fun' by importing women from further afield. They found taps that ran ink, chairs which collapsed when they sat on them, and other pieces of furniture which fell to pieces when they were touched.

Sandy had certainly succeeded in his no-expense-spared plan to humiliate women. Typically, he suffered little comeback. Nearly all his victims felt too degraded to complain.

*R*ecent figures showing the extent of wife-battering in the USA make grim reading: *6 million* wives and girlfriends are abused in any one year, and of these *2,000–4,000* women are beaten to death annually.

Sexual harassment can be found even in the most traditionalist and outwardly chivalrous institutions. A report prepared by female undergraduates at Oxford University and published in the students' newspaper *Cherwell* in 1983 listed 41 cases of sexual abuse by male lecturers and dons, including one case of rape.

The girls were too afraid to complain, said the report. A female don agreed that it was a major problem, even at dignified Olde Worlde Oxford: 'Women students are at the mercy of their college tutors. There is a ready market of vulnerable, innocent girls for dons to take advantage of their professional positions. They impose their sexual fantasies on their victims.'

*A*t an employment Appeal Tribunal in London in 1979, Mr Justice Bristow ruled that for a male employer to fire a woman because she was expecting a baby was not sex discrimination.

Dismissing an appeal by shop assistant Mrs Kim Turley, 20, of Battersea, against the refusal of an industrial tribunal to hear her case against Allders Department Stores, Ltd, Mr Justice Bristow said:

> When she is pregnant, a woman is no longer a woman. She is 'a woman with child', as the authorized version accurately puts it, and there is no masculine equivalent.

Also in 1979 came another historic decision in court, this time in Belfast, where Judge James Brown upheld a ban on 23-year-old Mrs Geraldine Collins from her local snooker club.

YMCA manager Michael Perrot had said that snooker 'wasn't a girl's game'. It called for strict silence, and

> in my experience it is impossible to impose silence for long on many, if not most, young girls.

The judge agreed with him:

> Your reasons are genuine and reasonable.

Asked why the Magic Circle, the elite body for British magicians, did not admit female members, their president, Francis White, said in 1982:

> We won't admit them because they can't keep secrets.

*I*n November 1984, after a lovers' tiff, salesman Dave Hawkins of Carlton, Leeds, decided to show his live-in girlfriend Wendy Latham, 24, who was boss. He put a notice in the local supermarket reading:

FREE TO GOOD HOME

LAZY WOMAN. CAN'T COOK. NAGS DAY AND NIGHT.

But will make coffee. Answers to Wendy. Phone . . . Ask for Dave.

The advertisement, nor surprisingly, brought no takers. Said Dave: 'It proves my point. I can't even give her away.'

> Sometimes I wish I was a housewife. Bloody easy life, isn't it? If my wife went out and earned some money, I'd stay at home and do the housework, no trouble. There are too many female chauvinist piglets in the world. They've got the answer all right: 'You go out to work, dear. I'll do all the dreary jobs like dust the video and play with the children.'
> *Comedian Freddie Starr*

*B*eing a 'forgotten' appendage of a successful husband, regarded as at best an ornament, at worst a millstone, is a common problem for American women. One member of the most heavily afflicted group—the wives of baseball-players—decided to do something about it.

Maryanne Ellison Simmons, wife of Milwaukee Brewers' catcher Ted Simmons, started a magazine called *The Waiting Room*, named after the squalid places where wives are made to wait while, after games, their husbands shower, have celebration cocktails, give interviews, and scoff the goodies at the buffet-table. She found a ready market, as women wrote in pouring their hearts out.

Wrote one wife: 'I am treated at worst as a nonentity and at best as a person who exists only in relation to my husband.' Complained another: 'I am a diversion to bear his three children and cart his electric toothbrush from coast to coast.'

Ms Simmons said:

> If a woman has her PhD in physics, has mastered in quantum theory, plays flawless Chopin, was once a cheerleader, and is now married to a man who plays baseball, she will forever be 'former cheerleader married to star athlete'.

A sex survey among teenagers in Los Angeles in 1980 showed just how ingrained male chauvinism is today. Of boys quizzed, 52 per cent said it was OK to force a girl to have sex in certain circumstances. More worrying: 42 per cent of girls agreed.

Friends of 'Wonder Woman' Lynda Carter told in 1982 how her husband, Ron Samuels, had been far from wonderful to her. He was said to have kept her a 'virtual prisoner', controlling whom she could see, where she could go, and what she could do. He allegedly put a time-limit on visits to her mother, wouldn't let her talk to other men (they were 'only out to exploit her'), and constantly told her that all her success was down to him as she was his 'puppet doll'.

After kicking him out, Lynda had to employ a bodyguard specifically so that her 'jailor' would not be able to return.

*A*nd finally . . . When a light plane piloted by a woman made a forced landing between the 17th and 18th holes at Washington's exclusive Burning Tree Club in 1983, the members knew the emergency procedure. They quickly called a cab to get her off the premises.

21 A Woman's Place

Women should remain at home, sit still, keep house, and bear and bring up children.
Martin Luther

*L*uther was only one of countless male sex-warriors down the generations to demand that a woman's place was in the home.

Nature intended women to be our slaves
. . . they are our property. They belong to us, just as a tree that bears fruit belongs to a gardener. What a mad idea to demand equality for women! Women are nothing but machines for producing children!
Napoleon Bonaparte

Men must go ahead . . . women must follow, as it were, unquestioningly . . .
D. H. Lawrence to Katherine Mansfield

My passions are soccer, drinking, and women, in that order.
Rod Stewart

My ideal woman is a 14-year-old deaf mute.
Peter Langan, London restaurateur

I ♣ my wife.
Response by TV comedian David Copperfield and others to those ubiquitous 'I ♥ NY' stickers

I don't particularly want to chop up women, but it seems to work.
Brian de Palma, film director, on cinema violence, 1984

There are only about 20 murders a year in London, and not all are serious. Some are just husbands killing their wives.
Commander G. H. Hatherhill of Scotland Yard, back in the 1950s

I'm just sorry that spanking is out of fashion now.
Ronald Reagan on the liberal lifestyle of his daughter Patti, aged 31

22 More Favourite Victims of Male Bludgeons, Blunderbusses and Brickbats

The script calls for her to answer the telephone. She sits to pick up the phone as her hair cascades down her back. Not bad. Kind of dramatic even. But then it is ruined.

She speaks.

Washington DC critic on Elizabeth Ray

Unsuitable Suitors

Glenda Jackson summed it up:

We still have these double standards where the emphasis is all on the male's sexual appetites—that it's OK for him to collect as many scalps as he can before he settles down and 'pays the price'. If a woman displays the same attitude, all the epithets that exist in the English language are laid at her door, and with extraordinary bitterness.

That was certainly what happened in the case of Elizabeth Ray, described by *Time* as a 'comely but shopworn blonde', in the case of the 'Washington sex scandals' of 1976.

Congressman Wayne Hays of Ohio was forced to resign after admitting that he had hired Miss Ray, who could not type, as his personal assistant 'for sex'. Another Congressman, John Young, of Texas, was implicated in the sex scandals but, while men were full of sympathy for Hays ('for a 64-year-old man he wasn't doing too bad,' Mr Edward Smith, over his gaspump back in Ohio, told *Newsweek*), it was Miss Ray who felt the full force of public anger.

Time compared her to 'Typhoid Mary'; Richard Reeves in *New York* magazine called her 'the pits'. Her ex-employer was said to have called her 'Exedrin' because she was such a headache, and the trial lawyer, Mr Charles Schulze, who became her boyfriend for a time, said:

If I took her out somewhere, I'd tell her not to say anything. Now and again she'd call me the next day to apologize.

As she felt the force of some of the most vicious publicity ever generated against a woman, she was refused a flat in a Washington condominium called Watergate West. The residents' committee said: 'We are afraid she will give the complex a bad name'!

The public vilification of Ms Ray was echoed in 1981 during a new round of Washington sex scandals: the victims this time were a group of women known as 'the flagrant five' and given press nicknames such as 'Flighty Fanne', 'Juicy Judith' and 'Lusty Liz'—collectively, 'the Scarlet Ladies of Capitol Hill'.

Of course, it's OK to be 'a bit of a lad' if you are a man; but if a woman enjoys sex with a number of partners then she's obviously a Messalina.

> For twenty minutes, a resident of Heath Road, Ripley, watched a couple having what appeared to be sexual intercourse in the back of a parked lorry. Then he and his wife complained to police about the woman's disgusting behaviour.
> *Report in the 'Derbyshire Times'*

*T*he same double standards applied during the abdication crisis of 1936, when any feelings that Edward VIII might have shown dereliction of duty were as nothing to those that Mrs Simpson was a fast, lewd and grasping woman.

When the news of her affair with Edward VIII first broke she was showered with abuse, hate-mail and death threats. Scotland Yard got a number of 'bomb calls'. Mrs Simpson received one letter addressed simply to 'King Edward's whore'.

So fierce were the attacks that she was forced to leave England for Cannes, and even there she had to be guarded by five Sûreté men. She said later: 'They never gave me one break. No one stood up to say, "Oh, stop it." No, people just got out their whips and lashed.'

> The King was once Admiral of the Fleet. Now he's just third mate on some American tramp.
> *1936 joke about Mrs Simpson*

> If he's going to pick up a jalopy, he should pick one with more mileage left in it.
> *Paris taxi-driver*

Women in Politics

Women in politics are treated first as a light diversion, second as a mild nuisance, and third, if they manage to break into a predominantly male world, as beyond the pale.

Much is made of David Ben-Gurion's famous remark to Golda Meir: 'You're the best man in my cabinet.' To male chauvinists, of course, this may seem the ultimate accolade. But Golda Meir hated the remark, and was not pleased when it was quoted back at her:

> You think it's a great compliment? What if Ben-Gurion had said 'All the men in my cabinet are as capable as a woman'?

Another time she said:

> I will never forget something that happened at a party congress in New

York in the 1930s. I made a speech and among the people listening there was a friend who was a writer. A man of talent and culture, outstanding. When I'd finished he walked over to me and exclaimed: 'Good for you! You made a wonderful speech! And to think you're only a woman!'

Those were his exact words, uttered spontaneously. It's lucky I have a sense of humour.

*B*ecause of her exceptional rarity, the female US politician faces even worse ridicule —witness Geraldine Ferraro. When Mrs Jeane Kirkpatrick was appointed President Reagan's special ambassador to the UN, the Chairman of the Senate Foreign Relations Committee, Senator Charles Percy, christened her 'the Unguided Missile'. And ex-Carter UN aide Brady Tyson snapped: 'I consider her appointment a real tragedy.'

*T*he prototype woman politician was, of course, Nancy Astor, who suffered something barely short of humiliation when she became the first woman to take her seat in the House of Commons. She wrote: 'Men whom I had known for years would not speak to me if they passed me in the corridors. They said I would not last six months. But I stuck it out.'

Elsewhere she recalled having once taken a petition round to a grocer named Boggs who had to have it slowly explained to him. He then agreed to sign it—but only on condition that no women were asked. He told her: 'That's right, Ma'am. Women don't know anything about these things.'

But perhaps the most pointed male put-down she endured was from a young American sailor she saw standing outside the House of Commons. Thinking he might enjoy being shown round by a famous politician, she asked: 'Would you like to go inside.'

His reply? 'No. You're the sort of woman my mother warned me against.'

*I*t is just as bad today, of course. No prizes for guessing towards whom these male arrows are aimed:

She appears to be perpetually late, harassed and in desperate need of a comb.
The Times

What a terrible toll the missed appointments, the uncaught trains, the dithering over important decisions have taken. Why, she is all too unhappily aware of what colleagues say now: that she would make a hash out of running a girl-guide outing, let alone a political party.

'Crossbencher', 'Sunday Express'

Have the voters of Crosby really gone soft in the head?

Auberon Waugh

Yes, Shirl's the girl. Shirley Williams—who auditioned for *National Velvet*, took up politics instead, and has become one of the most famous women politicians of the day.

But is it worth it? A few years ago she was designated 'Frump of the Year' by one Victor Fox, a London fashion-store boss. His unkind cut:

She is one of the very few women in the public eye who manage to make a day-dress look like a frock from 1945.

Or, as a Tory minister said:

She always struck me as a workhorse—and she dressed to look the part.

Women Newscasters

No single group of women has so made men fume, however, as the first female newsreaders. It is as if man's time-hallowed virility had been, at a stroke, nullified.

Pioneer female newscaster Barbara Walters told in 1984 how she felt out of place in a man's world. When Hugh Downs left the show, she was the senior figure—but they wouldn't let her take over.

For a day, yes. But if it's for a week, they bring a man in. I find that demeaning.

When we went to China with President Nixon, John Chancellor got asked about all the serious problems. I got asked about shopping! Afterwards, men complimented me on the way I'd worked in China, and told me: 'We thought we'd have to carry you.' Why? I've been on this show for *ten years*.

Mind you, the man kept making fun of Barbara—imitating her slight lisp, and referring to her all the time as Bwabwa.

Years earlier, in 1976, when she arrived at ABC, fellow anchorman Harry Reasoner threw a fit of pique about who should be given star billing. After things were patched up he admitted that he had said she was 'lousy' and had had his reservations, but said he was now ready to welcome her to the show. The compromise? Reasoner said things had been resolved in a 'non-sexist manner': the stars of the show would be announced 'by their surnames, in alphabetical order'.

It's been the same in the UK, of course:

That a medium so rich in its possibilities should have enfeebled itself by employing such as Miss Esther Rantzen is quite beyond me.

Tony Palmer

I can think of absolutely nothing to be said in her favour. As a measure of my dislike I can only say that when Esther and her grinning acolytes boasted how some con-man who they had exposed for the *n*th time had finally been sentenced to prison for two years I felt quite indignant and sorry for the poor fellow.

Richard Ingrams

And male TV chauvinists start young. When Angela Rippon was filming an outdoor opening sequence for soon-to-be-troubled TV-am, a little boy wandered up to her. She thought he wanted her autograph. In fact, he just wanted to improve her self-esteem by asking: 'Do you really go on TV with six inches of make-up on like that?'

Green and Common Women

A while ago, the *Daily Telegraph* quoted a young child telling his teacher he 'did not agree with these green and common women protesters'. The women who have camped outside US airforce bases, in some cases for years, in an attempt to change Britain's decision to deploy cruise missiles have stimulated a warlike response in many British males.

A Mr Alan Thomas wrote in a letter to *The Guardian*:

> Surely so many naive women have not gathered in one place since the 11,000 virgins of Cologne, who according to legend, set out on a pilgrimage and, being totally unarmed, were totally massacred by the Huns.

It's interesting to note that he couldn't get the legend of St Ursula *right*!

Their most persistent critic has been Mr Auberon Waugh, a critic and columnist, the thoughts of whom on the 'Green and Common Women' have included the following:

> The Lesbian army.

March 1983

> The Wimmin are all ugly and dirty and for the most part half-wittedly stupid.

April 1983

> The retreat from reason into some collective crypto-Lesbian infantilism.

January 1983

> After a while I begin to believe that their hideous, baggy, anti-nuclear trousers are irremovable . . . watching these foolish women as they lie around in their irremovable trousers trying to look like seal pups, I begin to understand the point of view which holds that nuclear war may be necessary . . .

Later he mused on a suggestion that the women smelled of 'wood smoke':

> Few people object to the smell of wood smoke. In my experience, the smell of the Greenham women is more like fish paste in the first instance, giving way to the meatier and more important aroma of bad oysters. Professional sniffers claim to find traces of the Wimpeyburger, onions, chicken shit and cabbage soup . . . At least we can be sure these possibly biological smells have nothing to do with sex.

Mothers-in-Law

Without doubt, however, throughout history the greatest vilification of a single identifiable group of women in the sex wars has been reserved for . . . mothers-in-law. That much exaggerated fear and trepidation, of course, goes up to the highest in the land:

> I don't feel as relaxed at Buckingham Palace as I do in my own home—but then, I don't expect anyone does when they visit their mother-in-law.
>
> *Captain Mark Phillips*

Courts over the years have heard just to what lengths man will go to silence his mother-in-law.

Bruce Irving, of Peterborough, Cambridgeshire, was given a seven-month suspended sentence and ordered to pay £500 in September 1984 after having knocked his mother-in-law to the ground, torn her clothes . . . and stuffed a pair of underpants in her mouth 'to stop her constant nagging'.

Jules Verdin of Paris was investigated by the authorities in 1983 after neighbours complained that his surburban home was overrun by mice. He said: 'My mother-in-law is terrified of them, and it's the only defence against her boring, interfering visits.'

A man in Worthing, Sussex, was so fed up with his mother-in-law exploding at him that he decided to get his own back—by blowing her up. He managed to plant explosives in her suitcase and prepared to send her on a holiday 'with a difference'. But the plot fizzled out. He was arrested after the police had received a tip-off.

Primo Canzoni of Florence was fined £25 for jamming his mother-in-law's bottom into a bucket after a family quarrel over where to spend their summer holiday. It took firemen three hours to free her.

An American man shoved his mother-in-law out of his car after a tiff and left her to the lions in a wildlife park at Carson City, Nevada. She was rescued by the people behind before the lions could eat her.

A desperate Arab crashed his car through the Israeli border and gave himself up to stunned Israeli troops. 'It's my mother-in-law,' said 33-year-old Hasam Aiyash. 'She nags from morning to night. But my wife insists on her being with us. I just can't stand it any more.'

Broughton Williams, a male nurse from New York, trained his Cairn terrier to bite his mother-in-law's ankles. The dog was rewarded with a toffee for every successful bite. Williams was fined £150 for assault.

Finally, Antonio Caitana was sued for divorce in Rome because his wife said he hit her mother on the head with the dinner whenever she visited. Unfortunately, the dinner was invariably in a heavy baking-tin at the time.

23 Classic Cuts

Nancy Astor
>The Polyanna of politics.
>*Harold Laski*

Mrs Patrick Campbell
>An ego like a raging tooth.
>*W. B. Yeats*

Bette Davis
>Down to her last thousand tantrums.
>*'Time'*

Queen Elizabeth the Queen Mother
>The Monster of Glamis.
>*Edward VIII, Duke of Windsor*
>
>The Dowdy Duchess.
>*Edward VIII again*

Jodie Foster
>A voice like raw meat.
>*Peter O'Toole*

Vicki Hodge
>That raddled, middle-aged trollop.
>*Sir John Junor*

Bette Midler
>An apache chief in drag.
>*William Marshall*
>The biggest thing in entertainment since the trap door.
>*Dermot Purgavie*

Patricia Nixon
>Artificial and plastic.
>*Prince Charles*

Elaine Paige and Barbara Dixon
>Look like Hinge and Bracket.
>*Jonathan King*

Lilli Palmer
>Poor dear girl, she was dropped on the head . . . at the age of 40.
>*Noël Coward*

Janet Street-Porter
>Voice like a foghorn.
>*Chris Kenworthy, 'The Sun'*

Gertrude Stein
>Literary diarrhoea.
>*Noël Coward*
>
>An old covered wagon.
>*F. Scott Fitzgerald*
>
>Just an old Roquefort cheese.
>*W. Somerset Maugham*

Elizabeth Taylor
>The only woman to drive a man to milk.
>*Richard Burton*

24 A Last Word on Women

*E*pitaphs, down the years, have provided a
final cruel example of just how much men do
hate their female counterparts.

Here lies the body of Sarah Sexton
She was a wife that never vexed one
I can't say as much for her on the next stone
> *Anonymous*

> **I laid my wife**
> **Beneath this stone**
> **For her repose**
> **And for my own.**
> *From an Ottawa graveyard (quoted*
> *by Nancy McPhee)*

Here lies my wife
Here lies she
Hallelujah!
Hallelujee!
> *Anonymous*

The talents in which she principally excelled
Were differences of opinion, and discovering
   flaws and imperfections . . .
She sometimes made her husband happy . . .
    But
Much more frequently miserable.
Insomuch that in 30 years cohabitation he . . .
   had not in the whole, enjoyed two years of
   matrimonial comfort.
    At length
Finding that she had lost the affections of
   her husband
   As well as the regard of her neighbours,
Family disputes having been divulged by
   servants,
    She died of vexation, July 20 1768
     Aged 48 years.
> *Anonymous*

Suggestions for Further Reading

It would be too space-consuming to list here the myriad of newspapers, magazines and books which have aided in the preparation of this volume. It may be helpful to the (male) reader who would like to delve into the subject of sex wars more fully, however, to list the works likely to best whet the appetite.

History

Balsdon, J. P. V. B.: *Roman Women*, Bodley Head, 1962

Flexner, Eleanor: *Centuries of Struggle: The Women's Rights Movement in the US*, Harvard, 1975

Harrison, Brian: *Separate Spheres: The Opposition to Women's Suffrage in Britain*, Croom Helm, 1978

Rogers, Katharine M.: *The Troublesome Helpmate*, Washington University Press, Seattle, 1966

Whitley, Elizabeth: *Plain Mr Knox*, Sheffington, 1960

Chauvinist Attitudes

Bullogh, Vern L.: *The Subordinate Sex*, University of Illinois, 1974

Figes, Eva: *Patriarchal Attitudes*, Stein and Day, New York, 1970

Hays, H. R.: *The Dangerous Sex*, Methuen, 1966

Korda, Michael: *Male Chauvinism and How It Works*, Barrie and Jenkins, 1974

Okin, Susan Moller: *Women in Western Political Thought*, Princeton, 1979

Biography

Guiles, Fred Laurence: *Jane Fonda: An Actress and Her Time*, Michael Joseph, 1981

Higham, Charles: *Kate: The Life of Katharine Hepburn*, W. H. Allen, 1975

Meredith, Scott: *George S. Kaufman and the Algonquin Round Table*, Allen and Unwin, 1974

Reed, Oliver: *Reed All About Me*, W. H. Allen, 1972

Teichmann, Howard: *George S. Kaufman: An Intimate Portrait*, Angus and Robertson, 1973

GET HER OUT OF HERE!

'The more I see of men, the more I like dogs'   *Madame de Stael*

'If he was asked, Chris Quinten would go to the opening of an envelope'
Jackie St Clair on the 'Coronation Street' star

'We cannot reduce women to equality. Equality is a step down for most women'
Phyllis Schlafly

'Before you meet your handsome prince you have to kiss a lot of toads'   *Graffiti*

'That's all England needs . . . another Queen who can't dress'
Joan Rivers on Boy George

*W*omen live up to their reputation for bitchiness in this hard-hitting collection of anti-men anecdotes and savage one-line put downs. But their venom is spiced with wit, and men too will enjoy the hits scored by such formidable females as Dorothy Parker, Raquel Welch, Germaine Greer, Jean Rook and Margaret Thatcher.

Illustrated by Bill Belcher

This book is dedicated to Lynne,
who has of course never shown any inhumanity to me . . .

Copyright © Graham Jones 1986

First published in 1986 by Century Hutchinson Ltd,
Brookmount House, 62–65 Chandos Place, Covent Garden,
London WC2N 4NW

Century Hutchinson Publishing Group (Australia) Pty Ltd,
16–22 Church Street, Hawthorn, Melbourne, Victoria 3122

Century Hutchinson Group (NZ) Ltd,
32–34 View Road, PO Box 40–086, Glenfield, Auckland 10

Century Hutchinson Group (SA) Pty Ltd,
PO Box 337, Bergvlei 2012, South Africa

Set in Linotron Sabon Roman and Bold by
Rowland Phototypesetting Ltd,
Bury St Edmunds, Suffolk
Printed and bound in Great Britain by
R. J. Acford Ltd, Chichester, Sussex

British Library Cataloguing in Publication Data
Jones, Graham, 1951–
    I don't hate men but . . . I don't hate
    women but . . .
    1. Sex —— Anecdotes, facetiae, satire,
    etc.
    I. Title
    306.7'0207   HQ23
    ISBN 0-7126-1205-X

Designed by Gwyn Lewis

I DON'T HATE MEN, BUT....

Graham Jones

CENTURY   LONDON · MELBOURNE · AUCKLAND · JOHANNESBURG

Contents

Preface
The Amazing Miss Gabor

*A*cid-tongued Zsa Zsa Gabor is probably the world's leading expert on men. She should be—she has married or at least been courted by most of the men in Hollywood. Among her brightest barbs:

> A man in love is incomplete until he is married. Then he's finished.

> You never really know a man until you have divorced him.

> I believe in large families. Every woman should have at least three husbands.

> I'm a wonderful housekeeper. Every time I get a divorce, I keep the house.

On first husband Burham Belge:
> . . . a moody, broody Oriental. He was 20 years older than me but it might as well have been 100. He was really 300 years behind me.

On third husband George Sanders:
> He never knew what he wanted to be—an English Duke, a beachcomber in the tropics, or the greatest woman-hater of all time.

On boyfriend Porfirio Rubirosa:
> He may be the best lover in the world, but what do you do the other 22 hours of the day?

On Felipe de Alba, whom she dismissed after eight days:
> He wouldn't even have made a nice pet.

Where Miss Gabor really excelled, however, was on a TV show called *Bachelor's Haven* where she read out letters from lonely hearts together with a crisp, no-nonsense Zsa Zsa reply.
> Dear Panel, My husband is a travelling salesman, but I know he strays even when he is at home. How can I stop him?

Her reply:
> Shoot him in the legs.

> Dear Panel, I am breaking off my engagement to a very wealthy man. He gave me a beautiful house, a mink coat, diamonds, a stove and an expensive car. What shall I do?

Her reply:
> Send back the stove.

1 Woman's Inhumanity to Man

As a creative crystallization of the movement beyond the state of Patriarchal Paralysis, this book is an act of Dis-possession, and hence, in a sense beyond the limitations of the label *anti-male*, it is absolutely Anti-androcrat, A-mazingly Anti-male, Furiously and Finally Female.
Mary Daly, US feminist

*P*oor men. That downtrodden, bedraggled army of the centuries. You don't believe me? Just listen to women on the offensive.

> Men have an unusual talent for making a bore out of everything they touch.
> *Yoko Ono*

> All men are rats. And those who aren't are boring.
> *Joan Collins*

> One hell of an outlay for a very small return with most of them.
> *Glenda Jackson*

Research by Roger Langley and Richard Levy in 1977 found that there were, in the USA, some 12 million battered *husbands*—with one-fifth of married women in the country confirmed or closet husband-beaters.

Langley and Levy's investigation began when a Washington policeman sought shelter in a woman's refuge claiming his wife gave him a ritual beating every Friday night. To their astonishment, they found that husband-beating was a widespread, serious and hitherto-undetected problem.

Said Levy: 'Most men are afraid to admit they are the victims of beatings. Not many men have the courage to face the snickers, innuendoes and open sarcasm inherent in this situation.'

*F*ew anti-male campaigns have scaled the heights of the one which took hold in the USA in the late 1960s under the title SCUM—the Society for Cutting Up Men.

Its message—that women can reproduce without men—came to the forefront of public attention when its organizer, Valerie Solanas, fired four bullets at artist Andy Warhol in his

Lower Manhattan studio. He was given only a 50:50 chance of survival after a bullet lodged in his back, and came off the critical list only after a four-hour operation.

Miss Solanas, who had had a bit part in Mr Warhol's film *I, A Man*, said: 'It is not often I shoot somebody. I did not do it for nothing.' She was later jailed for three years for attempted murder.

On the subject of violent retribution, could *you* name the famous Hollywood wife who threatened to sever her husband's private parts because of an incident involving the Queen?

No, it wasn't quite as bad as it sounds. But Mrs Alana Stewart made an extremely cutting remark in 1983 at a Hollywood party for the Queen. She wasn't too pleased to begin with to be separated from husband Rod, but became out-and-out mad on hearing him gleefully tell various distinguished guests about her displeasure. She was heard to remark:

If he continues telling people I'm furious not to be on his table, I'll cut off his tinkle and divorce him.

*N*ot that it never happens. In August 1985 Vailnaila Loisi, 32, was remanded in custody by magistrates in Sydney, Australia, after cutting off her sleeping lover's penis with a kitchen-knife. She then drove him to the casualty ward of a nearby hospital and dumped his severed manhood in a waste-paper basket there. A similar case in September 1985 was the fourth of its type recorded down under.

And then there was the wife who barbecued her husband . . . and calmly ate parts of his body, charcoal-grilled. In August 1984 Diane Fellman, 36, a hairdresser of San Jose, California, shot husband Elroy seven times at her salon; she then chopped up his body and took the bits to the couple's holiday cabin in a nearby forest. Neighbours remarked that the barbecue which she prepared 'smelled a little strange'.

She was convicted of first-degree murder after the jury had heard that her husband had become ill and that she didn't want to face having to look after him full-time.

Stella Walton, 45, killed her husband, too—but at their wedding reception. The groom slumped forward, dead, against the wedding cake at Stockton, California, in June, 1977, after the bride had stabbed him four times. She told police she was angry about the amount he had drunk at the post-nuptials.

And when Bill Holzapfel, 25, of Bradenton, Florida, ended his affair with Sandra Marich in 1983 she asked for one last kiss . . . and then bit his tongue clean off. She laughed and said: 'No other woman will want you now.' A court heard that he would never be able to speak normally again and was suing for damages.

*M*en are always on the receiving end—right up to the highest in the land. Male members of the Royal family, for example, are a 'soft' target

for the most vicious female tongues. Bette Midler once said unkindly of Prince Charles:

Boy is he rich, and boy is he ugly.

Even Princess Diana has been known to get in on the act, telling tennis star Chris Evert Lloyd that she couldn't persuade her husband to come to Wimbledon:

It's because he can never sit still. He's like a great big baby.

The Queen Mother has been known to display a mean anti-male streak. Once, when she was on a royal visit to South Africa, a Zulu broke through the police cordon and rushed towards her. She responded instantly, beating him about the head and body with her umbrella. Later she learned that he had been trying to present her daughter, then the Princess Elizabeth, with a ten-shilling note as a 21st-birthday present.

And the Queen has been known to show an occasionally impish sense of anti-male humour. After Bill Cleator, deputy mayor of San Diego, had outraged the Royal party and offended etiquette by putting his hand roundly on the Queen's back while conducting her around the city in 1983, he received an autographed picture of her with a thankyou letter from Buckingham Palace. It began: 'The Queen is very touched . . .'

*Y*es—women makes jokes against men. Have you heard, for example:

Men are like a North Sea ferry—roll on, roll off.

Living with a man is like living with a sex object—whenever you feel like it, he objects.

'Did that book you've just read have a happy ending?'
'You must be joking, she married him!'

My own favourite recent female quip comes from *Tube* presenter Paula Yates:

'Who does George Michael sleep with?'
'Nobody. You can't get two on a sunbed.'

One of the world's most celebrated chain letters showed feminist humour at its meanest. It read:

This letter was started by a woman like yourself in hopes of bringing relief to other tired and discontented women. Only, unlike most chain letters, this one does not cost anything.

Just send a copy of this letter to 11 of your good friends who are equally tired and discontented. Then bundle up your husband or boyfriend and send him to the woman whose name appears at the top of the list.

When your name appears on top of the list you will receive 16,877 men—and one of them is bound to be a hell of a lot better than the one you already have.

Do not break this chain . . . have faith.

One woman broke the chain and got her husband back.

At this writing, a friend of mine has already received 184 men.

Men who joke about women, by contrast, find themselves in the firing line for 'flagrant sexism'—or worse. For example, joking about 'the wife' can bring terrible retribution—as Woody Allen found to his cost in April 1967. Fed up with cracks like 'When I brought my first wife home my parents liked her but my dog died', 'She had that change of sex operation six times: they couldn't come up with anything she liked', and 'She's got everything in the divorce: if I remarry and have children, she gets them too', Harlene Allen, 25, sued her famous husband and NBC for $2 million for defamation.

*H*ell hath no fury, of course, like a woman scorned. Notable female avengers include Mrs Samuel Pepys, who pursued her lothario husband around the room toting a pair of red-hot tongs; and comedian Stan Laurel's second wife, who turned up at his third wedding screaming: 'Bigamist!' A woman at Alton, Illinois, found a nasty way of getting her own back on her husband, who had become a transvestite. When she died in 1984, she left him no money in her £68,000 will . . . but all her dresses.

But the real indignities suffered by men at the hands of women might never be known were it not for the divorce courts.

Warehouse manager Brian Shipley, 36, of Stafford, was divorced in 1981 after a judge heard that his wife Maureen had insisted he rush home from work to kill a spider. Another complaint was that she sent him back to work if he took a holiday and the weather wasn't fine enough. Mrs Shipley denied that it was unreasonable to ask him to come home and crush the spider: 'If he had not come and killed it, it might have turned up in another part of the house.'

A man from Dallas, Texas, was granted a divorce because of his 'ice-maiden wife'. She used to put ice cubes in his bed 'to cool him down when he got hot-blooded'. Another husband was granted a decree after he told how his wife smoked a pipe in bed . . . and twice set the bed-clothes on fire. And an elderly American divorced his young wife because she kept putting her 3ft pet alligator in the bath . . . while he was in it too.

Wilhelm Shultz, 41, of Stuttgart, was granted a divorce in 1984 because his wife Anna, 23, kept insisting her psychologist shared the marital bed 'so that he can interpret anything I say in my dreams'.

Sometimes it's the wives who complain. Ada Leonard, a New York striptease dancer, brought an action for divorce because she resented the fact that her husband didn't resent the fact she was doing the kind of work she was doing. (Got that?) And a Bermuda woman demanded a divorce on perhaps the most unusual grounds of all. She told the judge:

'Your honour, I have reason to believe my husband was not the father of my last child . . .'

Meanwhile actress Jane Wyman gave a succinct reason for divorcing one Ronald Reagan in 1948. She said simply:

He talked too much.

*A*s you can imagine, from the tongues of women have come, over the years, some pretty vicious barbs of invective. Bianca Jagger told Warren Beatty: 'So, we had an affair. You must be pretty bad. I don't even remember you.'

Some of the most erudite put-downs came courtesy of the celebrated razor-wit of Dorothy Parker. When a bore pestered her with his attentions in a bar in the 1940s, a time when she was blacklisted, she told him: 'With the crown of thorns I wear, why should I be bothered with a prick like you?'

My favourite showbusiness put-down came when bearded Elkan Allan, a producer for Rediffusion television, went on at great length to his secretary about what he should wear at a fancy-dress party. She finally replied:

Why don't you spray yourself with talcum powder and go as an armpit?

Showbusiness, you see, is a world of such *bitchery*. Witness model Jerry Hall, who launched into a bitter tirade in February 1984 against British male pop stars. On Boy George:

I keep hearing he's a big star but really he's a fat transvestite, isn't he? I don't see it can be healthy for kids to worship a fat transvestite.

On Wham! stars Michael and Andy Ridgeley:

Why do they get so excited about that band Bang!? You know, those two fat boys with streaks in their hair. The ones that look like girls.

Other women join the chorus:

That's all England needs: another queen who can't dress.
Joan Rivers on Boy George

He drove me crazy playing his own records all night.
Jill St John on Frank Sinatra

He may be the greatest actor in the world. But he's also the greatest arsehole.
Raquel Welch on James Mason

I'm in bed with Burt Reynolds most of the play. Oh, I know it's dirty work, but somebody has to do it.
Carol Burnett

*B*eware the sex-hungry female. The *Daily Telegraph* reported in June 1983 how a peasant in south-west China was having a quiet afternoon nap in a forest hut when suddenly in burst a tall, hairy 'wild woman' who proceeded to rape him. According to the Zhejiang provincial daily, 'He was too frightened to call

out and powerless to resist. The wild woman had sex with him for several minutes and then left.'

The story of 'wild women' on the rampage was confirmed by the Chinese magazine *Fossil*, which reported a number of cases of sexual harassment of the men living on the lower slopes of Mount Everest. The magazine told how, in 1972, a soldier disappeared while on patrol in Tibet. A few months later troops passing through the area heard a shout from a cave high on the cliff face. As they looked up, a man fell from the cave onto the rocks below. He was the missing soldier. His uniform was in shreds and his feet were tied with leather tongs. They saw above them a 'wild hairy woman with large breasts'—apparently his jailor, ravisher and torturer.

I've got to confess, though, that I have my doubts about these reports. Not so, however, about what is perhaps the most celebrated Western case of female sexual harassment. This came in 1975, when former beauty queen and vice girl Joyce McKinney followed Kirk Anderson, a Mormon missionary for whom she had developed an obsession, from Utah to London. With the help of an accomplice, Keith May, she knocked him out with chloroform, kidnapped him, and took him to a remote East Devon cottage. There he was chained to a bed with fur-lined manacles while Miss McKinney forced him to have sex with her a number of times over three days. He said later:

> After they tied down one leg and then the other, I could not resist the rest.

> There aren't any hard women, just soft men.
>
> *Raquel Welch*

> The more I see of men, the more I like dogs.
>
> *Madame de Stael,*
> *nineteenth-century French writer*

2 We Loathe Men!

The only problem with women is men.
Kathie Sarachild, US feminist

I hate men. They fill me with revulsion.
Violet Trefusis, lover of Vita Sackville-West

Patriarchy, that monstrous jock's joke, the Male Club that gives birth only to putrefaction and deception.
Mary Daly, US feminist

To call man an animal is to flatter him; he's a machine, a walking dildo.
Valerie Solanas, 'The SCUM Manifesto' (SCUM = Society for Cutting Up Men)

Grubby and distinctly grey around the underwear region.
Germaine Greer on [British] men

Sometimes I think if there was a third sex men wouldn't get so much as a glance from me.
Amanda Vail, 'Love Me Little'

I married beneath me—all women do.
Nancy Astor

Nothing really has changed since the Stone Age. Men still have the same mentality. If we all grew our hair they would probably drag us along by it.
Angie Best

Men hate independent women. Most of them think a woman's place is in the home. They show off their ladies, but then hate it if another man looks at her.
Faith Brown

Powerful men often succeed through the help of their wives. Powerful women only succeed in spite of their husbands.
Lynda Lee-Potter, journalist

Yes, men are foolish to expect us to revere them when in the end, they amount to almost nothing.
Pauline Reage, 'The Story of O'

. . . to aid men . . . SCUM will conduct Turd Sessions, at which every male present will give a speech beginning with the sentence: 'I am a turd, a lowly abject turd,' then proceed to list all the ways in which he is.
Valerie Solanas, The SCUM Manifesto

3 I'm No Man-Hater, But...

Women are aware that male superiority is a myth and
they deal with that knowledge in numerous ways.
Dale Spender

*E*ver been cleaned out? Even by Hollywood standards it staggered the male population of America in October 1983 when chat-show host Johnny Carson received a £146,000 *a month* temporary alimony demand from his ex-wife Joanna. He had offered her £11 million as a final settlement but she sobbed: 'Johnny, why are you so mean to me?' She told the divorce court indignantly: 'I have spent large sums updating my wardrobe in the past three years.' The court decided that £30,000 a month was enough to keep her going until the main hearing.

Meanwhile, Johnny joked on his show: 'I've just heard from my cat's lawyer. They're asking $12,000 a week just to keep him in gourmet cat food.'

The eventual settlement *was* that original £11 million—£3.5 million in cash, plus their £2.2 million Californian mansion, three apartments in New York worth another £2 million, £25,000 a week alimony, a Rolls, a Mercedes and a Datsun, jewellery, half Johnny's pension, a Picasso . . . and 75 Krugerrands. Gulp.

*W*omen rape men, and ravaged males deserve to be protected, insisted John Lee, barrister and Labour MP for Birmingham Handsworth. They should be safeguarded from 'lustful, over-sexed and physically strong women', he said, urging the then Home Secretary, Merlyn Rees, to change the law so that women could be tried for rape. Mr Lee, 50, said that although he personally had never been despoiled he knew it could be 'as harrowing an experience for a man as for a woman':

> The present state of the law is based merely on the respective characteristics of the female and the male.
>
> But there can be no doubt that a woman can rape a male, particularly if she is big and buxom and it is a puny youth. There have no doubt been many instances where this has happened and the law cannot be invoked.

And he added:

> Certain women could easily overpower some men and satisfy their own sexual cravings in a way in which, if a man had

been the predator, a charge of rape would have ensued.

*I*n April 1983 rock producer Felix Pappardi, 41, who helped mastermind such classics as 'Strange Brew' and 'World of Pain' was shot dead after an argument by his wife Gail. She told police: 'He came home late.'

Glynis Yoxall, of Barnsley, Yorkshire, was placed on probation for two years for malicious wounding in May 1981 after admitting hitting her husband over the head with his Bullworker until it shattered.

A major blow against the US male came in 1983 when psychologist Cynthia Silverman of Los Angeles began a course for wives in how to cheat their husbands. At her academy of adultery they were taught these basic rules for cheating on a man: first, remember to cover absences with excuses that can't be checked; second, never confess or admit anything; and third, always choose a married man for a fling—he's got as much to lose as you have if the story gets out.

*W*hile Barbra Streisand was married to Elliot Gould, she went to a premiere with Omar Sharif. Gould demanded to know why. 'Because the ticket would have cost me 250 dollars,' she replied.

Miss Streisand showed how she likes men to be at her beck and call with her amazingly insensitive treatment of her European press agent after she had come to London for *Funny Girl*. He sent a car to meet her with the regretful message that he could not be there in person: he had married that day and was having a one-night honeymoon before devoting his all to her affairs.

That was not good enough for Barbra: she phoned him in his bridal suite and demanded his instant presence. He was closeted with her for several hours going over her publicity campaign, while his young bride was left alone . . . on her wedding night.

The press agent, by contrast with Miss Streisand, was the model of decorum. He said: 'You have to admire someone who is so dedicated to her work.'

> When I overheard two women talking recently, a cold shiver ran up and down my male spine. It seemed that the father of one of them had just died and the other said: 'Yes I understand how you feel. It's not like losing a husband. You can replace him but you can't replace a father.'
> *Letter in 'Woman' magazine*

One of the most destructive comments ever made against a man came from the lips of Miss Mandy Rice-Davies at a magistrates' hearing during the Profumo scandal of 1963. Asked by counsel if she was aware that Lord Astor had denied her statement that she had been to bed with him, she replied, with innocent precision: 'Well, he would, wouldn't he?'

The phrase passed into the language.

Actress Raquel Welch is a firecracker with a vicious left hook, says film-producer Patrick Curtis. He tells the story of how she 'flattened a guy twice her size':

> Once, when we came out of a movie in Los Angeles, she found her Jag hemmed in. When she tried to get out, she bumped into the car behind. This guy got out and started screaming at her. Suddenly she slugged him right round the jaw.

*B*eware of the aggressive career woman: in 1983, a team from the University of North Carolina warned that husbands of high-achieving working wives face a *three times* greater risk of heart disease than if they themselves are the breadwinners. No, it isn't the extra housework. The university researchers say it is something to do with the professional women staggering home from a hard day at the office and passing on the stress of their jobs.

Prince Anne showed her hatred of those macho male press photographers during a trip to East Africa in the 1970s. The gaggle of paparrazzi, she noticed, were standing rather close to some lions packed in wooden crates. One of the great cats stretched out a paw and tried to grab itself a meal—one of the press photographers. A game ranger shouted a warning. The snappers, thankfully alerted, jumped away.

In no uncertain terms, Princess Anne told off the ranger.

Another unkind cut: As part of Nancy Reagan's campaign against drug abuse, spouses of heads of state from around the world were invited to a conference in the USA. Spectacular in his absence: Mr Denis Thatcher. 'Flagrant sexism,' observed the New York Civil Liberties Union.

The *Daily Telegraph* reported in May 1984 a new twist to those ubiquitous FRANK—LIZ windscreen visor stickers: in Cornwall a car with the slogan 'MASTER—SLAVE' was spotted. The vehicle was driven, reported the *Telegraph* somberly, by a woman.

*J*ust before a women-only nude scene during the filming of *She'll Be Coming Round the Mountain* in 1984, a phone-called came to the studio manager, apparently from the actors' union Equity. It said that a new 'anti-sexist' rule had been passed that, for every woman who took her clothes off on the set, a male technician must do the same. There was some trepidation among the all-male film-crew, but eventually they decided that 'orders is orders' and stripped off to the buff. They went through the scene, goose-pimples everywhere.

Only when the girls started to fall about with laughter after the order to 'print!' had been made was the naked truth revealed. It had been a practical joke by actress Julie Walters and her feminist friends.

My wife gave me a load of hand-forked manure for the garden on my birthday. After 30 years of married life, I was anxious. The comments from my friends were guarded. Tell me what you think—in confidence. Write Box L. 1725.

Advert in 'The Times', London

*F*lowers, romance, soft music. It used to be easy for a man to woo his lady-love. Not so nowadays. Musician Andy Stowell of Ealing was set 12 'labours of love' when he attempted to win the heart of Beverley Moody, a 19-year-old English student at Oxford University whom he had met at the Proms. The full list of tasks was:

1 Drink champagne from a virgin lady's shoe
2 Feed your tropical fish
3 Leave home
4 Read *Crime and Punishment*
5 Get a letter published in *The Times*
6 Write a book and get it published
7 Learn your multiplication tables up to 25
8 Persuade your brother to get his hair cut
9 Win an international conducting competition
10 Get an invention for a bassoon patented
11 Become 'Housewife of the Day' on a BBC radio programme
12 Teach your grandmother to sing 'The Stately Homes of England'

Lamented Andy, 23, who *did* succeed in becoming 'Housewife of the Day':

I wrote a letter to *The Times* but they didn't publish it. I'm trying to teach my grandmother to sing 'The Stately Homes of England' but she hasn't got a good memory and keeps lapsing into 'All Good Things Around us Are Sent from Heaven Above'.

But the real trouble is I don't know any virgins.

Said Beverley ungraciously: 'I hadn't planned on giving him any reward even if he completes all the jobs—and I doubt whether he'll manage that.'

Female chauvinist Dawn Newbold of Clay Cross, Derbyshire, set a town gasping in December 1973 when she put an advertisement in a newsagent's window. It read:

Free to a Good Home. One husband, hardly used. House-trained.

After being ribbed by his workmates, who'd seen the card (he hadn't), Trevor Newbold rushed home from work demanding an explanation. Later he complained:

It's not true I'm 'hardly used'. I do a fair bit of cooking and cleaning up.

4 Savage Put-Downs

Overbearing and stupid. He talks like the character he plays.
The man totally believes his own publicity.
Joan Collins on Larry Hagman

I t has to be said. In the sex wars, when it comes to a razor-sharp tongue, to absolute bitchery, a woman would put a hundred men to shame.

Take Brooke Shields, whose speciality is 'seeing off' unwanted admirers. One of them was ageing crooner Julio Iglesias—'the Spanish tummy'—who, at her 18th birthday party, pursued her relentlessly, ending his spiel by asking if he could have her hand in marriage.

Said Miss Shields coldly: 'Can I introduce you to my mother?'

And Shelley Winters tells the story of her unkind cut at a show-business party to a stranger who seemed vaguely familiar. She chatted patiently with him for several minutes while struggling to recall where on earth she'd met him before.

Finally he put her out of her misery. 'I'm Tony Franciosa,' he said. 'I'm your ex-husband.'

H ow cruel can you get? Traffic warden Julie McGeogh approached a gleaming Mercedes at Royal Ascot to tell the driver to move off a pedestrian crossing. In the car was Ringo Starr. 'I know you!' she cried: 'You're Max Bygraves.'

Ouch! Some more examples of women at their most waspish:

Warren Beatty
He's like jelly. He comes into your life, gives you a taste of himself, then drifts past.
Viviane Ventura

He had spots, wore glasses because he was practically blind without them, and was never happier than when he was on the phone.
Joan Collins

George Best
We had dinner and he tried to get me back to his apartment that night. But I didn't

want to know—he was too old and didn't have much conversation.
Joanne Latham

David Bowie

I talked and talked about doing a movie with him. But who wants to make a movie with a guy who's prettier than you?
Bette Davis

Peter Bowles

I've never met anyone so conceited or so foul.
Beryl Reid

Richard Burton

[Face to face] I do believe you would screw a snake if you had the chance.
Joan Collins

David Frost

My idea of boredom is a night out with him. He giggles at everything you say. And I don't want some guy earnestly stroking my hand all evening laughing every time I say something quite ordinary.
Jill St John

Richard Ingrams (of *Private Eye*)

I'd rather interview a rat. At least they spread the plague and make no bones about it.
Diana Dors

Simon Le Bon

As much talent as a bucketful of congealed custard.
Daniela Soave, 'Sunday Mail'

Nick Nolte

[Face to face] I hear you've been drunk in every gutter in town.
Katharine Hepburn

Burt Reynolds

The kind of guy who would stop on his way down the aisle to say hello to a pretty girl.
Tammy Wynette

Omar Sharif

He's not sexually attractive to me. He's too old.
'Sleeping Prince' co-star Debbie Arnold

Rod Stewart

His trouble is that he has never grown up . . . and never will.
Ex-wife Alana Stewart

John Taylor (of Duran Duran)

There was real love in what he was doing, which made up for his lack of ability.
Kiss-and-tell model Samantha Phillips

5 A Kick Where it Hurts — Favourite Targets for Female Demolition: Show Business and Pop

Ol' big nose is back. If he was on the beach you would kick sand in his face.
Adella Lithman on Barry Manilow

The successful showbusiness male is a magnet for women. Women without scruples. Women after cash, chasing a life among the bright lights, seeking reflected glory, or maybe wanting a chance to vent their spleen on all men through the medium of someone well known.

Make no mistake, it's a jungle out there—and the good, old-fashioned, red-blooded male is losing.

The cruellest case recently of a grasping woman taking over and dominating a male Hollywood idol was that of Groucho Marx, who in the later years of his life was drugged and subjected to physical abuse by hired companion Miss Erin Fleming. She was eventually sued by the Bank of America for $1.4 million for allegedly milking the star—who died in 1977, aged 86—of much of his estate.

John Ballow, who worked for Marx as a chef, said that Miss Fleming once told him: 'You only get one chance in life to succeed. Meeting Groucho was a stroke of luck and I'm going to make the most of it.' He testified that Miss Fleming struck, cursed, and threatened Marx in his final years, and forced him to entertain against his will.

The jury in Santa Monica awarded damages against her of £320,000.

One of the worst humiliations Hollywood males have to suffer, of course, is 'kiss and tell', when former wives and girlfriends, often egged on by big-money rewards for 'digging the dirt', return in print to haunt them.

Anna Kashi, first wife of Marlon Brando,

gave *Penthouse* this cruel catalogue of invective against the man regarded by millions as a top sex symbol:

> As a seducer, he's clumsy. As a lover, he's inconsiderate . . . His technique showed all the subtlety of a guillotine. His scale of emotions lacks the grace notes. If he were not a film star, I doubt that he would get to first base with women.

Brenda Arnau depth-charged the lusty reputation of dashing Hollywood actor and playboy George Hamilton in 1983:

> He really fancied himself as a ladies' man but when it came to having sex with him, it was quite a comedown.
>
> He spent a lot of energy telling me how great he was going to be—he is a very good superstud talker. But when it comes to making love, he is vastly over-rated. It was short and not so sweet.

To be a man in Hollywood is to become part of a human zoo where every hair, every muscle, every gold-filled tooth is pored over in detail to see if it passes the girls' sex-symbol test. Listen to this on Victor Drai, French boyfriend and svengali of Jackie Bisset:

> He was wearing skin-tight white jeans, his face was spotty, his teeth needed urgent dental care, and worst of all, he had bad breath.

That from the *divine* Miss Janet Street-Porter, every inch a beauty herself.

But it's all too easy for a woman to knock the superstar off his pedestal with a few choice and venomous words. David Frost's intending bride, Lady Camilla Fitzalan-Howard, was asked by a relative whether the transatlantic TV presenter was religious.

'Yes,' she replied: 'He thinks he's God.'

Oona Chaplin rejected Ryan O'Neal's passionate advances with the cruel rebuke: 'I don't go out with little boys.' Barbra Streisand refused to comment on Robert Redford's performance in *The Great Gatsby* on the grounds that if she couldn't say anything nice she'd better not say anything at all. Gitty Milinaire said of a brief fling with Omar Sharif: 'I did not enjoy our lovemaking. Once was enough.' While Victoria Tennant, costarring with Robert Mitchum in *The Winds of War*, said: 'One day he was so weak that when I threw myself into his arms, I knocked him over.'

> I was not surprised to read that Terry Wogan has the largest ears on television. They are simply in proportion to the size of his head.
>
> *Mrs Jean Jackman of Bournemouth, letter in the 'Daily Express'*

*O*h yes, and then there are those female fans. They'll never leave a man alone.

Burt Reynolds, who suffered for years from hypoglycaemia, told how once, after a particularly nasty attack, he was rushed to

hospital in a coma. Recovering consciousness, he found himself in the intensive-care unit in some discomfort, with tubes coming from his nose and an intravenous drip in each arm. The first nurse who found him awake was full of concern. 'Oh Mr Reynolds, now you're awake at last I *must* have your autograph,' she said. Well, he might have died on her, and *then* what would she have had to show the girls?

Worse happened to pop idol Paul Young. In June, 1985, he was actually hauled off the stage by a screaming horde of girls, suffering bruises, a jarred back and a dislocated rib. The incident happened in Melbourne.

> I reached out to touch a girl's hand and the next thing I knew I was flying through the air. As I scrambled back on stage they got hold of my shirt and tried to rip it off my back. It left a scar on the side of my neck like a burn mark.

He added that the next night 'the rib kept popping out, so I had to come off between numbers to get it put back into place'.

Still in the pop world, in February 1985 poor Simon Le Bon was invited by Princess Stephanie of Monaco to her 20th-birthday dinner. In the middle of the meal—at the fashionable Atmisfare restaurant and night-spot in Paris—the Princess suddenly went into a sulk and disappeared. Simon was left to pick up the £2,000 tab for the indulgence of 15 famous guests.

*W*hat Hollywood men have suffered at the hands of their leading ladies!

Mae West gave her 'two bottles a day' costar W. C. Fields a torrid time. After he had promised he would do 'anything' to work with her she ordered him to be deprived of drink on the set, which made him nearly suicidal until he succeeded in smuggling in some liquor and . . . got drunk.

Miss West was no respecter of reputations. She called for a studio crew and issued the famous order: 'Pour him out of here.'

One-time 'James Bond' George Lazenby told how Diana Rigg made love-scenes rather unpleasant for him by chomping garlic shortly before their screen embraces. According to Robert Mitchum, though, the most difficult leading lady to play against was buxom Jane Russell, with whom he shared many a steamy clinch. He said: 'She was a really pleasant lady. In the kissing scenes she'd pop her chewing gum up your nose.'

*N*o wonder they called her 'bossyboots' and 'the headmistress'. When breakfast-TV new boy Nick Owen made his debut at the side of Miss Angela Rippon the atmosphere was all-acid. (She was eventually relieved of her post.)

If there was any sexual chemistry between the two it was obviously going to produce high explosive. A typical exchange:

Miss R: Do you like Roland Rat?
Mr O: Yes I love the laugh. [Laughs like Roland Rat.]
Miss R: My goodness, that's terribly good. Do it again.
Mr O: [Laughs like Roland Rat again.]
Miss R: Well, you're nearly as good as him. Maybe you should go up there and he would come in here to replace you.

A male colleague confessed: 'She really has become a monster. She wants to be treated as Number One.' So don't be taken in by all those soft armchairs.

Trainee Turkish wrestler Bette Midler holds the TV-am record for bagging, and almost debagging, a brace of British TV chat-show hosts, Bruce Forsyth and Michael Parkinson—though, to be fair, she did not succeed in her avowed intent of removing the trousers of either of them.

In 1979, on *The Bruce Forsyth Show* she spent much of the interview wrestling on the floor with the balding, grimacing Mr Forsyth. She then moved on to a scrap with the BBC's Michael Parkinson. Parkinson said:

> She wanted to take my trousers off so she could take a look at my legs. She didn't shock me at all even though she did try to take my clothes off.

Not that even that matches Miss Midler's performance at the Golden Globe awards in Hollywood in January 1980 when, among other outrages, she sallied forth to Dustin Hoffman's table and told him to 'eat shit'.

*A*nother TV comedienne on the offensive was Pamela Stephenson who in November 1985 made a successful attempt to debag TV-am's Nick Owen. After being told he had been named one of the world's most boring men she yelled: 'I'll make you more interesting' before yanking off his trousers. Mercifully she stopped when she reached his striped Y-fronts cooing: 'I was only trying to brighten him up a bit.' But all the excitement put poor Mr Owen's back out and he had to be replaced for a time by another presenter, Henry Kelly.

*W*ho would slug Frank Sinatra with all those heavies around? Well, Shelley Winters did. Let her tell the story:

> At about three in the morning Frank flew into a terrible rage at me. And, despite my gorgeous hat and white gloves and elegant navy dress, I screamed like a fishwife and slugged him. Sinatra just slammed into his limousine and roared away. Maybe he went home and hit Ava Gardner.

Of course, parting is not always such sweet sorrow. Cher seemed to get on quite well with husband Sonny in the old 'I Got You Babe' days. But then things changed. She claimed that working with him was 'slavery' and tried to sue him under the 13th Amendment for subjecting her to 'involuntary servitude'.

The blow of Cher's becoming involved with other men wasn't exactly softened for poor old Sonny. She told him, when she was seeing millionaire record tycoon David Geffen, 'There's one thing I know. I've been out with a real man.'

And Sonny confessed that it was 'a real downer' when, one night when they were in bed together, Cher turned over and called him by the wrong name.

Back to Mrs Joanna Carson (turn to page 9 if you dare), a name to send shudders through all men contemplating escape from matrimonial imprisonment. In November 1983, when the final noughts were being added to one of the largest divorce settlements in history, Mrs C was heard making observations about her husband's future career.

'Johnny,' she said, 'has been signed up to compere the Oscars next year. And the Oscars are going to get their highest ratings in history.'

'Oh, how do you know that?' asked her companion.

'Because,' said Mrs C, 'when I get through telling all I know about Johnny, everyone in America will tune in just to see what he looks like.'

As a famous male face you can of course be innocently minding your own business in a bar . . . and the next moment some woman is trying to make a name (or money) for herself at your expense. This happened to *Coronation Street* star Chris Quinten on a trip to the Mediterranean in the summer of 1985, when 17-year-old holiday-maker Emma Lane poured her drink all over him. The picture that followed became front-page news back home in Britain.

Insult was well and truly added to injury when in the caption Mr Quinten was described by Emma as 'a short, boring wimp'.

A subsequent article gave vent to the views of another aquaintance, model Jackie St Clair, who said:

> He thinks he's wonderful. His line in chat is so corny his opener to me was a super-sophisticated 'Your place or mine!'
>
> I looked at his boots and told him that *I* liked to be the half of the couple wearing high heels.

She added that only 'new girls in town' could be impressed by Mr Quinten:

> The rest of us get tired of seeing him popping up at every do going. If he was asked, Chris Quinten would go to the opening of an envelope.

6 You Must Be Joking

Bigamy is having one husband too many—monogamy is the same.
Anonymous

So you think that's funny. Sure, this is sex wars: women have a savagely humorous streak. Any excuse is a good excuse for poking fun at and belittling those poor bedraggled males.

Making love with a man is like a ride on the Waltzer. You climb on, it's over real quick—then you want to throw up.

A Dorset driving instructor asked his female pupil: 'If a traffic signal changes to amber only, what will you see next!'
   'That's easy,' she replied. 'Some fool man trying to beat the lights.'

I was out one night with a girl friend who told me: 'You'd better hang on to him.' I didn't realize she meant that after two drinks he falls down.

'What are you getting for your husband this Christmas?'
   'I don't know. Make me an offer.'

You must have heard about the wife who got rid of ten stones of unsightly, unwanted flab in three months. She divorced him.

'I don't know what happened,' the steward told the young wife on a Miami-bound plane. 'We left your husband behind at Gatwick airport.'
   'Thank heavens!' exclaimed the woman. 'I thought for a moment you were going to say my baggage.'

Woman: Do you and your husband like the same things?
Friend: Sure, but it took him 12 years to learn.

Wife: My husband's just run off with the au pair.
Friend: That's too bad.
Wife: Yes, now I've got to do the ironing myself.

'He was so depressed, he went and put his head in the gas oven.'

'What did you do?'

'Oh, I basted it every 15 minutes.'

The grey-haired old lady smiled sweetly at the couple who were locked in a passionate clinch at Victoria Station. The young woman wept as the man boarded the train, leaving her all alone on the platform.

The old lady went over and tried to console her. 'I suppose you're crying because you have to leave your husband.'

'Hardly,' she replied. 'I'm crying because I have to go back to him.'

*A*mong the most successful stand-up women comics on the club and holiday-camp circuit is raucous blonde Pauline Daniels, of Ellesmere Port, Cheshire. Some of her gems:

My husband came home half drunk last night. He'd run out of money.

I call my husband the Loan Ranger. He's always looking in my bag for silver.

'Quick, quick,' I told him as he came into the kitchen, 'I want you to make mad, passionate love to me.'

'Why now?' he said.

'Because I want to time this egg. I don't like them to boil longer than 27 seconds.'

7 Acid Repartee

Edna, you look almost like a man.
> *Noël Coward to suit-clad Edna Ferber*

So, my dear Noël, do you.
> *Edna Ferber to Noël Coward*

Instant suicide! Here's a collection of man's greatest verbal lashings . . . when he rashly dared to take on a woman at her special subject. And lost, of course.

> I've spent enough on you to buy a battleship.
> > *Prince Albert to his mistress Lillie Langry*
>
> And you've spent enough in me to float one.
> > *Lillie Langry to Prince Albert*

> Can you imagine anything worse than being in bed with Omar Sharif and finding it not exciting any more.
> > *Russell Harty to Diana Dors*
>
> Yes, being in bed with you and finding it was.
> > *Diana Dors to Russell Harty*

Richard Burton was once thrown a lavish birthday party by his lady-love of the time, Princess Elizabeth of Liechtenstein, and was extremely rude to her. The next day he cabled her:

> WHY DO WE HURT THOSE WE LOVE THE MOST, AND I DO MEAN YOU?

She wired back:

> BECAUSE YOU'VE HAD SO MUCH EXPERIENCE, AND I DO MEAN YOU.

After she asked him why he had been so unpleasant to her when she first came to Westminster as an MP, Winston Churchill told Nancy, Lady Astor:

> I felt as if I had been caught in a bath by a woman and had not even a sponge to defend myself.

She replied:

> Don't be ridiculous, Winston, you're not

nearly handsome enough to have worries of that kind.

Other vials of acid:

> Say Missus, how many toes are there on a pig's foot?
>> *Heckler to Nancy Astor*
> Take off your boots, man, and count for yourself.
>> *Nancy Astor in reply to heckler*

> May I congratulate you on being the only man in your team?
>> *James Callaghan to Margaret Thatcher*
> That's one man more than you've got in yours.
>> *Margaret Thatcher to James Callaghan*

> How would you cope if a crowd of hefty dockers were to turn on you?
>> *Party chairman to Dr Oonagh McDonald at selection Meeting*
> I'd try not to be too violent.
>> *Dr Oonagh McDonald to party chairman*

> I can't bear fools.
>> *Anonymous date to Dorothy Parker*
> That's queer, your mother obviously could.
>> *Dorothy Parker to anonymous date*

And here are two memorable put-downs to hecklers. From female impressionist Faith Brown:

> The last time I saw a mouth like yours, Lester Pigott was riding behind it.

And from one of the famous singing sisters, Maureen Nolan:

> Let's you and me do a duet of 'Swanee River'. I'll sing it and you can jump in it.

MY ORGASMS ARE MY BUSINESS

8 Savage Sisterhood: Women on the Warpath

Men have been left to their incredible destruction and incompetence long enough.
Beverley Skinner, Bristol Women's Liberation Group

If any man doubts that the shock troops are being mobilized to crush him in the sex wars, he should make a quick recce of women's writings today. One thing is certain—he's going to be stunned by what he reads.

> We know what a boot looks like
> when seen from underneath,
> we know the philosophy of boots . . .
>
> Meanwhile we eat dirt and sleep; we are
> waiting under your feet;
>   When we say Attack
> you will hear
> nothing at first
>   *Margaret Atwood, 'Song of the*
>   *Worms'*

An urban guerilla group called 'Direct Action' scored a number of successful strikes on male targets in 1982. When a car full of dynamite planted at the Litton Systems plant in Toronto, which makes parts for cruise missiles, exploded, several men were maimed for life. The group also blew up an electricity-transmission station and on Canada's west coast fire-bombed a store selling 'sexist' videotapes. What really got the organization into the papers, however, was when the leader of the gang, Ann Brit Hansen, 30, threw a tomato at the (male) judge who had sentenced her to life imprisonment.

Phyllis Chester has observed that since the penis is the proof of male existence, the proof of male power, it is too important and too vulnerable an organ to be exposed publicly, especially to women. Male and female viewer alike may

respond with embarrassment or dismay at its diminutive size. Women may feel cheated, as if the terrorist who has held them hostage and threatened with the pistol in his pocket, turns out to be armed only with a finger!

Sarah Kent, 'Women's Images of Men'

You've seen them on the attack in the House of Commons; at the Miss World contest; against Wimpy Bars. Yes, and a remorseless campaign by feminists resulted in one man from Bath being forced to shut down his restaurant. Mr Richard Williams, 34, had adopted a 'St Trinian's' theme for his bistro, with waitresses in gymslips and school desks for dining tables. Women objecting to the 'sexist' image of the restaurant forced its closure in December, 1983, after pouring glue into door-locks, painting slogans on the windows and making a succession of anonymous threatening telephone calls.

*R*efused permission to join the sacred Gorsedd circle of the white-robed male druids of Pontypridd in May 1979, women claimants hatched a novel plot to humiliate the men. Using National Eisteddfod notepaper, they sent an official invitation to the Chief Druid at Pontypridd, asking him to travel to Cardiff, where the Pontypridd druids' application to be represented among the revered Gorsedd bards (a signal honour) was to be considered. Mr Gareth Gregory, the Chief Druid, and his followers arrived at the appointed meeting-place at Cardiff College of Education only to find the committee room they were directed to was . . . the ladies' lavatory. After a long wait inside, the druids returned to their cars which they found had been painted with the slogan: 'Come back in 15 years.'

Mr Gregory denounced the hoax as 'female chauvinism of the worst kind', and said that it would ensure their exclusion for at least a further 25 years.

Men don't wash their hair often, don't care whether they have hair in their ears or hair sticking out of their noses. To me it is quite revolting.

Germaine Greer

We cannot reduce women to equality. Equality is a step down for most women.

Phyllis Schlafly

A conference for lesbians organized by the London group 'London Friend' in November 1984, called for the ultimate ostracism of men—from the cradle to the grave. They demanded removal of 'heterosexist' teachers, and came up with what delegates insisted was a 'serious, sensible, and reasonable' plan for 'all-women cemeteries'. One newspaper observed: 'Some of them wouldn't be seen dead with a man.'

Madam—I hope I was the woman who 'curtly and coldly informed' Richard Gott (author of 'A Man of Greenham', 15 December) 'in the strident tones of extreme feminism that men were supposed to be at the Orange Gate by the Creche.' It was a privilege.

Letter in the 'Guardian' (Jill Bennett of Manchester)

One tactic adopted by a women's group was to have cards specially printed—looking like business cards—to hand to male recalcitrants. On one side the cards read: 'You have just insulted me as a woman. How would you feel if somebody did this to your sister or a friend?'

The reverse said, 'This card is treated with a special chemical. In three days your prick will drop off.'

I like the idea of Women Against Violence by Men. Women against Violence is too wishy-washy altogether, but Women Against Violence by Men puts the blame squarely where it belongs, the rats.

Lesley Garner, 'Mail on Sunday'

1 If your man is late for tea, do you:
a) bang the plate down to show your displeasure?
b) smile, after all he's probably had a hard day at work?
c) chop his willy off?

From a quick quiz, 'How Assertive Are You?', in the magazine 'Mancunion' (sic), quoted in 'Private Eye'

Q: How do you get 16 elephants into a mini-car?
A: Simple—you seat 8 in the front and 8 in the back!
Q: How do you get 16 giraffes in?
A: You can't . . . it's full of elephants!
Q: How do you get 16 men in?
A: Ask the elephants to get out quietly. Inject each man with a tranquillizing dart. Bind ankles and wrists with strong twine. Remove seats, engine and shopping from vehicle. Whilst wearing sterilized gloves heave bodies in, using sledge-hammer to ram into place. Use plenty of woman power to lean on doors, bonnet and boot to close. Lock up. Leave 12 hours (have a party) for drug to wear off, then all (elephants and giraffes included) stand around jeering and laughing!!!

'Manchester Women's Liberation Newsletter', quoted in 'Private Eye'

9 Men: Faulty Merchandise

Women have many faults
Men have only two
Everything they say
And everything they do.
Anonymous

Women go to so much trouble yet accept
a man's pot belly, warts, bad breath,
wind, stubble, baldness and ugliness.
Germaine Greer

Men are marvellous when the house burns
down or the children fall dead—the big
crises. But they're absolutely hopeless
with small things like when the toast is
burned or the dog is sick on the carpet.
Barbara Cartland

The true male never yet walked
Who liked to listen when his mate talked.
Anna Wickham, 'The Affinity'

Behind almost every woman you've ever
heard of stands a man who let her down.
Naomi Bliven

A hard man's good to find—but you'll
mostly find him asleep.
Mae West

Never trust a husband too far nor a
bachelor too near.
Helen Rowland

Men are like naughty little boys. They
always want the bar of candy they can't
have. When they've got it at home, they
go out and look for another piece.
Jackie Collins

A man's home may seem to be his castle
on the outside; inside it is more often his
nursery.
Clare Booth Luce

Many simply lack the basic skills of
communication in some important aspect
of their lives, be it at work, at home, with
others or by themselves.
Anna Ford, 'Men'

How to tell if your husband is
lying—look and see if his lips are moving.
Anonymous

The trouble with some women is they get
all excited about nothing—and then
marry him.
Cher

10 Sex Sirens, Sex Strikers

I wanted to be an actress and a scholar too. My first move was to get a Rolling Stone as a boyfriend. I slept with three then decided the singer was the best bet.
Marianne Faithfull

Now to the real sex wars! Sex is a weapon used relentlessly by women to gain the upper hand with men. *How* varies widely—from lurid sexual molestation or, yes, even rape, to complete bans on sexual contact in order to force a man to come to heel.

GO GETTERS

Research at Yale University by Dr Philip Sarrel, published in July 1981, showed an 'alarming' rise in the number of cases of men being raped by women. Many were left physically and emotionally scarred and deeply ashamed, he reported, and many showed 'severe after-effects'.

The case of one young male medical student was among those cited. He was tied to a bed by a female student who threatened to stab him with a scalpel if he didn't have sex with her. He was so terrified, wrote Dr Sarrel, that he was afraid to go out with women and have sex with them for two years.

A middle-aged man, raped at gunpoint by four women, was so overcome by shame and guilt that he refused to give evidence against his captors.

Sarrel, a director of Yale's sex-counselling programme, said: 'When a woman rapes, it is not a sex act. It is an act of anger and an act of power.'

In 1983 police in Florida were called to rescue a 22-year-old man who had been raped at gunpoint by an attractive blonde.

He had been walking down a palm-lined avenue at Fort Pierce one Saturday night when a sleek white Lincoln Continental had pulled alongside. The driver—described as in her early 30s, with long fingernails and wearing only diamond earrings and a beach robe—had asked him if he wanted a lift. When he refused she had pulled an automatic pistol and forced him into the car.

A police spokesman said: 'She drove him to a

wood and forced him to strip. Then she put the pistol to his head and made him indulge in sexual acts.'

The victim, who was not named, was said to have been 'terrified'. He told officers: 'She could have pulled the trigger at any time and left me lying there.'

*T*hree American psychiatrists reported in 1972 that so weighty had the sex demands of the typical woman become that there was a wholesale increase in cases of impotence among males who felt guilty at being unable to satisfy their womenfolk. The report, in the GPs' journal *Pulse*, referred to the 'insatiable' demands of liberated women, noting that 'Young people [i.e., men] are being pressured into intercourse'.

One student was quoted as saying:
> When you get one of these liberated women into your bed, you damn-well better perform the way they want or that's the end of the relationship.

A 41-year-old woman GP from Long Island, New York, was accused in court in August 1981 of paying to have a middle-aged Manhattan physician dragged and delivered to her so that she could make love to him. Dr Rochelle Konits was said to have told a district attorney's office official: 'I'm not going to hurt him. I'm going to kill him with love.'

Mr Denis Dillion, county district attorney, said that Miss Konits had failed in her attempts to hire a gunman and so had chosen the drugs-and-kidnap route.

When two undercover agents telephoned her and said they had drugged him, she told them: 'Good, bring him to me, and I'll tie him up.'

She pleaded not guilty in Nassau district court to charges of conspiracy and misuse of a drug. She said from home: 'I didn't do anything wrong. I didn't hurt anybody.'

She admitted to having once had a relationship with her averred victim but added: 'We were never close.'

*E*rrol Flynn told of how he had once accepted an invitation for a late-night drink from a Russian Princess in New York's St Moritz hotel. After two bottles of champagne she invited him into the bedroom. After the first bout, there were 'murmured soft tones of a self-satisfied male, and little whimpers in Russian from her'.

But Round Two brought a scream of pain from Mr Flynn, who 'seemed to have been bitten by ten scorpions'. He clutched at his buttocks and found blood on his hands:
> She held in her hand a brush with a long handle and prickly, hard hairs, possibly steel. At the propitious moment of our engagement—to employ a euphemism—she brought it down with all her force on my bare arse.

Mr Flynn said he made himself scarce after that:

> She might have got it into her head to whack me in the head next—or some other sensitive spot.

*T*wo professions are top of the list for sexual harassment by women: clerics and medics.

Church Ministers A pressure group called 'Broken Rites' has had to be formed in Britain to combat the rapid increase in divorces among the clergy. Among case-histories was that of the parson's wife who was horrified to discover that her husband was having two affairs simultaneously behind her back. Secretary Mrs Pauline Morrell said:

> It has been hushed up for years but clergymen are pursued by predatory women. They are seen as a challenge, but they also tend to be very sympathetic, imaginative, caring sort of people who women relate to easily. Being only human they respond.

Doctors A special report in the GPs' magazine *Pulse* in 1972 warned about surgery seductresses. In particular doctors were told to watch out for the 'ivory thigh' syndrome, whereby a female patient 'contrives to give the GP tantalizing glimpses of her ivory thighs or her rosy-tipped bosom'. Doctors were advised to swot up on their 'body language' in order to be able to read the danger signs early. 'There is the intimacy of the doctor's touch,' the report

warned: 'It may have fantasy overtones for some.' Doctors were alerted against 'failing to respond to previous signals, which gives the impression of playing hard to get which is encouraging the patient to play even more games'. Newly divorced women, said the author of the report, Dr Patrick Kerrigan, 40, needed to be particularly watched.

*N*ew York, of course, is the mecca of the sexually aggressive—or should we say predatory—female. In December 1984 a survey by Princeton sociologists established that, for every 100 single women in the Big Apple, there are 63.1 single men. 'Phooey,' blasted the swinging singles (female branch):

> There aren't even 63.1 single men in the whole of New York City!

Who would be a beautiful, intelligent, witty, level-headed, generous 30-year-old girl-about-town with a successful career and her own apartment? 'Once you've counted out the homosexuals, loons, joggers and workaholics, and culinary freaks, who is there?' complained one woman to a newspaper. 'With the workaholics you become another meeting on their schedules, joggers are either running or tired, and guys who cook all the time are dead boring.'

A new craze was reported in 1983 in New York—trawling the bus-stops. Other tactics were: (a) the noting of car registration numbers, which are then run through a computer by a

friend in a government department and swapped with other man-hunters; and (b) 'shopping lists', whereby girls are encouraged to add details and addresses of single men they know to a mailing list which is then swapped between predatory sisters.

*B*ette Midler's manager Aaron Russo has told this story of the sexual aggressiveness of the star:

> She was unhappy. She rang up and said: 'I must have your body.' I went over and then she said: 'God, you're so fat, you'd better be my manager instead.'

It is an occupational hazard for male sex symbols, of course. Action-man actor Lewis Collins told how a German brunette tried to foist herself on him in a hotel bar one evening and simply refused to take 'no' for an answer.

He was waking up the following morning when he felt a tap on his shoulder. It was the German girl. Although naked, he firmly ushered her out of his room, then went to take a shower. Suddenly, he heard a tapping at the shower door, and the girl burst in and grabbed him by the face. 'I may have a tough-guy image, but I just don't think this is fair,' he moaned.

Omar Sharif found himself at the mercy of an even more determined female in his motel bedroom one night in Dallas, Texas. When he refused her entreaties to make love to her, she pulled a revolver from her handbag and ordered: 'Take off your clothes!'

He said: 'I stood in front of her, my knees shaking, and told her, "Madame, you can see it's quite impossible." She did see.' His unconventional last line of defence against the 'love me or die' ultimatum had worked and she left.

One persistent female admirer made the life of an Italian professor a misery. He had to call in the police no less than 73 times to assist in countering her lusty advances. The woman, a 28-year-old student, was so besotted with him after having first seen him on a train that she even spent the night on his doorstep. But the last straw came when she bit him and then attempted to take a chunk out of the policeman who called to investigate the crime.

*S*exual harassment comes in many curious forms. Cheeky barmaid Linda Blackie lost her claim for unfair dismissal in March 1983, after the landlord of the White Swan, where she worked, described how she had a penchant for molesting customers by tweaking their nipples.

Landlord's son-in-law Kevin Flexham told the hearing in London about one evening when 34-year-old Linda became merry behind the bar: 'I went to try and steady her up, but she turned on me and tweaked my nipples in full view of the customers.'

Darts player David Smith added: 'She grabbed my nipples and started doing the same to all the other lads in the team.'

Divorcee Linda, of Wickford, Essex, said: 'I

tweak men's nipples for a laugh, just to be friendly. I'm sure the regulars will miss me now I'm gone.'

And police at Reading, Berks, in July 1984, admitted that they had little to go on in the case of a phantom female flasher who had been terrorizing local menfolk. She was described as 'stunning, wearing a red plastic mac, with nothing underneath except knickers, red satin stockings and suspenders'. Every time she confronted a victim, she would throw open her plastic cape to reveal an expanse of naked flesh.

A police spokesman said that what made things worse was that all the attacks happened in broad daylight.

SEX STARVATION

Woman's other great weapon in order to force a man into line is, of course, to deny him sexual favours—either choosing the most appropriate moments or altogether.

In 1983 a husband told a divorce judge in Varna, Bulgaria, that he had to make a written appointment with his wife every time he wanted to make love to her. Husband Andrew would make the request in the morning before leaving home, and, if it were granted by his wife Irina, he was allowed to spend part of the night in the marital bed. But, if she left a note saying that she had a headache, the bedroom door remained locked and he had to sleep on the couch.

Washington was rocked in January 1985 by the revelation that the highest-placed woman in the land, 53-year-old Secretary of the Human Service Margaret Heckler, a member of President Reagan's cabinet, had denied her husband John, 57, sex for 22 years. In an eventual divorce-court tussle over the family fortune, Mr Heckler said that he had remained married to his ambitious wife to avoid a scandal which would have harmed her political career. He had been condemned to a life 'of celibacy or adultery', said his lawyer, Edward Nev.

In 1972, there was the case of a wife who, complaining of her husband's 'excessive sexual appetite', said that only under two conditions would she be prepared to continue living with him: (a) no cooking, and (b) no sex. But James Buckland, 46, of Stoke Newington, agreed to these proposals, made by his wife Kathleen at the London Divorce Court. 'If he wants her back on those terms, he wants her back rather strongly,' observed Mr Justice Ormrod.

My girlfriend and I were in love and were thinking about getting engaged. Then her father bought her a horse for her birthday and she has not seemed the same since.
Letter in *Woman's Mirror*

32

11 A Kick Where it Hurts – Favourite Targets for Female Demolition: Male Royals

Before you meet your handsome prince you have to kiss a lot of toads.
Graffiti

To hear some women talk, however, *all* princes are toads, frogs or newts in any event. Perhaps the most savage diatribe against a royal son came in March, 1984, when *Daily Express* 'first lady of Fleet Street' Jean Rook set about Prince Edward in swashbuckling style. Some samples:

This priggish, and often astoundingly pompous prince . . .

Since he first publicly opened his megamouth—as he's now been dubbed for his brawling discourtesies at cameramen through a megaphone—Edward has always been a little bleater.

He whined about coverage of his brother Andrew's affair with Koo Stark . . . he whinged to come home after only six months' teaching in New Zealand.

Though his GCEs were below average, he still crawled over the academic wall around Cambridge—with all the momentum of a slow-growing ivy.

There's no fool like a young princeling . . . stripped of his lucky birth, Edward is an undistinguished lad with no obvious potential for being anything but the Duke of Somerset.

He could at least be publicly pleasant, since it's about the most he has to offer the world.

It's tougher still being Prince of Wales. Remember the Australian model, Bree Somers, 22, who foisted herself on Charles in the surf at Bondi Beach in 1981? That was the tour where Australian girlhood welcomed him unkindly

with placards reading, in a belittling reference to the royal ears: 'HELLO, WINGNUT.'

Poor Charles may be rich and famous, but he has at least twice been rebuffed in no uncertain terms by women, to name but Anna Wallace and Lady Sarah Spencer. The latter said: 'I wouldn't marry anyone I didn't love, whether it were a dustman or the King of England. If he asked me I would turn him down.'

He had had his bad moments with Princess Diana. Most people by now know her nickname for him: 'Fishface'. And during their honeymoon she threw a bucket of water over him one time when he was boarding the Royal Yacht *Britannia*. The officers respectfully greeting his arrival did not quite know where to put their salutes. Again, she put him down in no uncertain terms in September 1985, when he chatted backstage with some young dancers after a charity show at Hadde House, Aberdeen. He asked them: 'Do you do a lot of barre exercises?' The princess immediately stepped in with: 'You are the expert at that, dear.'

Other males have felt the sting of her tongue. When three-year-old Adam Wallford sniffed at her bouquet of freesias and roses and told her they were 'yucky', she responded: 'Typical man!'

*B*ut Charles is lucky by comparison with earlier Royals. George IV's wife, Caroline of Brunswick, used to make wax dolls of him, give them horns, and then set about stabbing them with pins before finally flinging them in the fire. During the 1770s George's brother, the Duke of Clarence (later William IV) was kept firmly in place—in Bushey Park, to be precise—by his mistress Dorothea Jordan, a leading popular actress of the day. He allowed her £1000 a year but his father, George III, told him this was too extravagant, and ordered him to reduce it to £500 a year.

She sent her response in the form of a playbill, at the bottom of which was printed: 'No money returned after the rising of the curtain.'

Nor have women shirked from criticizing the royal male personage. George IV (again) was described by Georgina, Duchess of Devonshire, thus: 'He has a figure which although striking is not perfect. He is inclined to be too fat and looks too much like a woman in men's clothes.' George I came in for worse. The Electress Sophia called him 'The Brunswicker who is "faut doux" and makes his mother love him because he is so ugly'. Elizabeth, Duchess of Orléans, observed of him: 'The Elector is grossly selfish, shy and deceitful—suspicion, pride and avarice make him what he is'; elsewhere she remarked upon his 'odd cranium'. Lady Mary Wortly Montagu went further: 'In private life he would have been called an honest blockhead, and fortune which made him king only prejudiced his honesty and shortened his days.'

*P*erhaps the most regular victim of womens' wiles over recent years has been Prince Andrew. He became embroiled in an embarrassing affair with an actress, Koo Stark, who had appeared in 'soft porn' movies, and was also the victim of a sordid £40,000 'kiss-and-tell' exclusive in a Sunday newspaper after accepting the attentions of Miss Vicki Hodge, ex-lover of a jailed killer. She said later: 'I set him up.'

The worst episode, though, was his exploitation by a seedy Holborn restaurant specializing in the caning of customers by waitresses dressed as schoolgirls. Sonia Moore, 21, was said to have told him: 'You've been a naughty boy. I'm going to give you six of the best. You were told not to come here and here you are.'

The *Daily Star* gave a 'blow by blow' account of how Sonia, described as a '21-year-old leggy brunette', caned the royal bottom: this started off tastelessly and became, well, less tasteful. It concluded: 'It's the first time I've whacked a Royal bottom and it will probably be the last. Still, it was good fun. He didn't mind at all.'

It was all a pack of lies, of course, and later an apology was made to the Palace by the phantom flagellists.

*T*hough probably the unkindest feminist cut against a prince came in February 1984, when 11 female West German MPs issued a statement saying that Prince Charles should be sterilized—'to take a great physical and mental burden' off the shoulders of Princess Diana.

12 Ads Up — The Writing's on the Wall

If you catch a man, throw him back.
Graffiti·

Women do bite back! And if you need any more proof of their reply in the sex wars, look at the 'male-dominated' world of advertising. Just think of those poor, underpaid, male executives, their campaigns—and careers—ruined by cruel swipes of the feminist brush. A series of postcards produced by the Women's Press, London E1, captured the best for posterity.

A 'Clairol Nice 'n' Easy' poster, advertising hair colorant, showed a girl by a tree on which was etched: 'JW = BW.' The slogan read: 'Renew His Interest in Carpentry.' The female graffitists added their own response:

SAW HIS HEAD OFF.

'Isn't it time you changed sweet nothings into somethings?' bleated an ad for diamonds placed by the jewellery trade.

GIVE HER YOUR PAY PACKET

scrawled the merciless feminists. And, most devastating of all, an ad for 'Pretty Polly' tights, captioned 'Where would fashion be without

little pins?' (i.e., legs), was annotated boldly:

FREE OF LITTLE PRICKS . . .

It's not just in advertising, of course, that woman has done her worst with the Dulux. A memorial in a south-coast town recalled the Battle of Hastings with the inscription: 'In 1066 near this spot the Normans landed and were repelled by the men of Romney.' Wrote a feminist underneath:

AND SO AM I.

Some other pearls of feminist wisdom appended to walls around the world:

I LIKE THE SIMPLER THINGS IN LIFE—LIKE MEN

WHEN GOD CREATED MAN, SHE WAS ONLY EXPERIMENTING

SO WHAT'S UNUSUAL ABOUT A MAN WALKING ROUND SAYING HE'S THE SON OF GOD?

THE WALTZ WAS INVENTED BY
MEN—FOR THEM TO LEAD AND STEP
UPON WOMEN AT THE SAME TIME

HE MAY HAVE HAIRS ON HIS
CHEST—BUT SO DID LASSIE

THE DIFFERENCE BETWEEN THIS FIRM
AND A CACTUS IS THAT THE PLANT HAS
PRICKS ON THE OUTSIDE

A WOMAN WHO ASPIRES TO BE EQUAL TO
MEN LACKS AMBITION

I ALWAYS TOUGHT MEN WERE A
PHALLUSY

I USED TO FIND HIM BORING—UNTIL I
STOPPED LISTENING

A WOMAN WHO THINKS THE WAY TO A
MAN'S HEART IS THROUGH HIS STOMACH
IS AIMING A LITTLE TOO HIGH

IT BEGINS WHEN YOU SINK INTO HIS
ARMS—IT ENDS WITH YOUR ARMS IN HIS
SINK

A WOMAN NEEDS A MAN LIKE A FISH
NEEDS S BICYCLE

A WOMAN'S WORK IS NEVER DONE . . .
BY MEN

13 Wild, Wild Women on TV

As Pug Henry in *The Winds of War*, he is a fine tribute to the embalmers' art. Like an overstuffed sofa in naval uniform, I'm convinced that he is wheeled around on castors.
Nina Myskow on Robert Mitchum

They're bold, they're brash—and they're the most brutal purveyors of feminine arsenic since the ark. Today's Fleet Street TV columnists—virtually every one a woman—leave no reputation spared in their quest for new depths of abuse to pour on their unfortunate—almost inevitably male—victims.

You'll need a strong stomach for this chapter.

Christopher Biggins
In his sugar pink suit last Sunday he looked as scrumptious as a big, fat fairy cake.
Judy Wade

John Denver
Drippy John had made it up with his wife Annie after a three-year separation. She, of course, was the subject of the appalling 'Annie's Song'. Let's hope their reunion doesn't inspire a follow-up.
Sheila Prophet

David Dimbleby
I detest him. I'm incensed by his plump opinion of his own self-importance. By his smug self-assurance that his pseudo-intellect is even bigger than his head. By his puffed-up hair-do. By the way in which, even if your TV set is at eye level, he appears to be talking down to you.
Jean Rook

John Forsythe (Blake Carrington in *Dynasty*)
So wooden he looks like something to hang your hat on.
Maureen Paton

Tom Jones
He swaggered on stage as if he were at the OK Corral forcing his granite voice into his stomach.
Moira Petty

Brian Keith (of *Hardcastle and McCormick*)

The thing that worries me is his varicose veins, clearly visible in the scenes where he insisted on wearing shorts. His legs could take a nasty knock in one of those punch-ups or car chases. His wig could get dislodged, too.

Margaret Forwood

Barry Manilow

The singing stick-insect . . .

It took three cushions to get Manilow's bum on Tarbuck's leather sofa. Then he proceeded to prove once again that he has no intention of saying anything interesting, or giving us any real insight into his personality.

Margaret Forwood

Nick Owen

. . . He said he was picked to replace David Frost because he was ordinary. I've been watching you, Nick, and you are. But I'm not sure it helps any.

Hilary Kingsley

Chris Quinten

What a bore . . . not a lot going on up there.

Jean Ritchie

David Soul

However he became a sex symbol defeats me . . . The guy is so completely lacking in personality that he always looks as if he's sent himself, rather than his shirt, to the dry-cleaners.

Maureen Paton

If one of these most vicious of vicious women stands out it is the self-styled 'Queen of the Box' Nina Myskow, whose frightening wide-eyed visage stares out each week from a page in the *News of the World*. Her column, which invariably includes some hapless male being dubbed 'Wally of the Week', has out-McEnroed McEnroe. Among Nina's nuggets:

Ronald Allen (**David Hunter of** *Crossroads*)

Woodentop.

Anthony Andrews (**after nude TV scene**)

My willy of the week. To be fair—chilly willy. I'd have written more if there'd been more to write about.

Charles Aznavour

He topped the bill—difficult in his case without a stepladder. He's so small, he's not so much a frog as a tadpole.

Max Boyce

Without wishing to antagonize the Welsh, please explain *why* do you find him funny? As far as I'm concerned you've got me snookered. Boyce is merely a load of old balls.

Gyles Brandreth
A posh cleverclogs, his silly posturing cannot mask his utter lack of charm.

Joe Bugner
How I longed for Ali—anyone really—to button Joe Bugner's lip on the Russell Harty show . . . the dazzlingly dense sporting dummy (you'd have a tough job guessing which has more padding—his head or his gloves).

Cannon and Ball
Last time round, I said Cannon and Ball should be shot. That's much too good for them. And much too fast. No, what they deserve is something tortuously tedious, absolutely excruciating, and not at all enjoyable. Just like their show . . .

Richard Clayderman
Creepy and Cheesy.

Paul Cola
A knitting pattern who has just learned to speak. (Pity about the dropped stitches, dear.)

Lewis Collins
Flabby and feeble . . . SAS? Soppy and sappy.

Gary Glitter
Grotty old Gary looked more like Terry Tarnished than ever. His dilapidated features seemed permanently congealed in a blank look of cretinous surprise (I suppose once he raises those eyebrows his forehead furrows get trapped under his wally-like wig). He used to be loveable in an OTT sort of way. Now he has as much charm as an unwashed armpit.

Tom Jones
Excruciatingly embarrassing . . . toe curling . . . rusty . . . Most undignified for a grandfather. I believe women throw knickers at you. I toss you a truss . . . just a small one . . .

Henry Kelly
Here's an anagram for you—ITT. A right one.

Matthew Kelly
The big, bearded, wet-lipped twerp from *Game for a Laugh* looks as if he put gay into Game. Raise a laugh? He can hardly raise his wrist. The limp wimp . . .

George Michael and Andrew Ridgeley of Wham!
If there were screams, they were screams of laughter . . . Called to announce the top female singer of the year, Bill and Ben

turned out to be this year's Woodentop Men.

Ben—who looks not unlike Benny from Crossroads—opened his blubbery lips and shoved his trotter straight in his chops with 'the best female singer of 93'.

Brilliant, boys, brilliant! Accomplished with all the flair and appeal of a lump of slimy pork-substitute luncheon meat, well past the sell-by-date.

Handsome hunks? Meat-heated chunks. SPAM!

Bob Monkhouse

The BBC have struck oil—gallons of it—gushing every time Mr Monkhouse opens his mouth. Slobbery Bob . . . in the showbiz sandwich, you are the filling. Ham. Greasy ham.

Sam Neill

Not since Eric D. (Dipstick) Morley oozed on stage at the Miss UK contest have I seen so much hair-oil on a man.

David Philpott (TV-am's weatherman)

Stuffing him into a sweater, calling him a matey 'David' and sending him out to be just as pompous outdoors in Camden Lock is not enough. What you have to do next chaps, is shove him in the canal.

Oliver Reed

This male chauvinist pig once hogged the limelight with his boozing and womanizing. Now he's old and stone cold sober, he should stick to his sty.

Ted Robbins (comedian)

Bobbing up like a grotesque barrage balloon on Saturday afternoons . . . plodding and ponderous, he looks like a defective blancmange stuffed into trousers. Dazzlingly untalented . . . devastatingly charmless . . . a loser if ever I saw one.

There is just one role for which he is perfectly suited: at kids' parties. Blindfold them, give them a pin, and a tail, and make this pain in the bum bend over.

14 Grounds for Divorce

The marriage suffered a setback in 1965 when the husband
was killed by the wife.
New Law Journal

*N*owhere do you see a woman's callous,
vindictive and violent side better revealed than
in that battleground of the sex wars, the divorce
court. Brace yourself!

François Malondra, chief air-traffic controller
at Nice airport, was certain that his wife Colette
was deceiving him. So he hired a private
detective, Serge Petremann, to gather evidence
for a divorce. Petremann soon reported that
Colette had at least three lovers—a big blond
Swede, a French casino croupier and a
basketball-player—each with their regular day
for spending two or three hours at the
Malondras' villa overlooking the Bay of Angels.
Under French law, however, Colette had still be
confronted in the arms of her lover in the
presence of a lawyer and a policeman.

The trap was sprung the next time the Swede
called. The husband, detective, lawyer and
policemen all burst in . . . and found Colette
quite by herself and extremely angry at the
intrusion.

Petremann and the witnesses raided the villa
again when the basketball-player called. Once
again Colette seemed to be all alone. But the
private eye had tumbled to her ploy. Striding
over to the grand piano, he threw open the lid
to find . . . the curled-up form of the
basketball-player, wearing only his underpants.

The divorce went ahead.

*H*yper-henpecked husband Herbert Fenner,
57, of Cheam, Surrey, lived in the *dining-room*
because of his bullying wife, a divorce court
heard in 1983. Sometimes she would chase him
around the house, lashing out at him with
tea-towels. On other occasions she punched
him in the face, and once she threw him
downstairs. For good measure Mrs Fenner, 49,
denied her husband sex—as well as refusing to
cook, mend, sew or do anything else for him.

But she didn't stop at that. When he left the
dining-room haven where he lived and slept, the
Mayor and City of London Court was told, she

would turn off the radiators and open all the windows to make life as uncomfortable as possible for him when he came back. He was forced to take tranquillizers, and eventually was driven from the house altogether.

Mr Fenner was granted a divorce because of his wife's 'violent, unreasonable behaviour'.

*H*am Nelson, married for six years to Bette Davis in the 1930s, issued one of the most comprehensive lists of all time of 'unreasonable behaviour' by a wife. He claimed in his uncontested divorce action that she was 'so engrossed in her profession that she neglected and failed to perform her duties as a wife'. That was just for starters.

She had, he said, been 'inattentive, cruel and distant to the point of rudeness and embarrassment'. During their time together she had 'insisted on occupying herself with reading to an unnecessary degree'. And when he asked for 'conjugal friendliness and affection', she had 'become enraged and rude' and indulged in 'a blatant array of epithets and derision'.

Poor Ham went on that she would upset the household, and unnerve and humiliate him. She would not go out with his friends and, when he brought them to the house instead, would ignore them, 'read intently in their presence', or try to humiliate them.

Mr Nelson added that Miss Davis was not present at mealtimes; she would not go on vacation with him, preferring the company of her mother; and even, on one occasion, when they had agreed to a holiday, she suddenly took off elsewhere with her sister. She talked incessantly to acquaintances about how 'unstable' their marriage was, saying that she didn't want to go on living with him and hoped he would leave her alone with her work and her family.

The deposition ended by saying that Miss Davis had 'spoken to him so bitingly and caustically, her comments were so cruel' he had finally left her for good.

It was all quite mild really: he never even mentioned her affairs with William Wyler or Howard Hughes.

*O*ne unfortunate American husband came out of jail after a 10-year sentence for armed robbery to find his wife had given birth to four children during his absence. Astonishingly, the judge ruled that this did not constitute adultery and denied him a divorce.

In July 1975, Judge Victor Orgera of the New York State Supreme Court ruled that there might have been opportunities for conjugal relations during the 10-year sentence, either if Mrs Margaret Walker had slipped into the jail or if her husband had slipped out. Judge Orgera did not accept prison records stating that Mr Walker's wife had not visited him once during his 10 years 'inside' and that he had never been 'out'.

Mr Walker said he wanted a divorce decree

so that he could marry again. Mrs Walker was later contacted by reporters—too late for the divorce case—and yes, just in case you're wondering, she admitted that none of the children was her husband's.

A husband sought a divorce in Sydney, Australia, after his wife told him following their wedding that she had only married to win a bet with a girlfriend. 'I suppose one can expect in this jurisdiction always to hear new stories about human behaviour,' said the judge.

Another man whose honeymoon didn't last long was Thor Isbister of Copenhagen, who issued divorce proceedings against his wife Sonja, in 1984, following her boast that she had tried out all his six brothers as sexual partners before accepting his proposal.

Yes, sex can be a problem for newly-weds. A 68-year-old just-married bride recently complained to the London Divorce Court that her 78-year-old husband, an arthritis sufferer, failed to fulfil her expectations of a healthy sex life. Poor dears.

*R*idiculously suspicious wife Gay Digby turned the family home into a 'Fort Knox', a court heard. She locked all the internal doors of her 14-room mansion in Purley, Surrey, and hid the keys from her husband Gerald, after accusing him of stealing semolina from the pantry. She also locked the doors on any sex life for him, saying it might bring her out in a rash.

Mrs Digby, 51, was so suspicious that she used to complain that the zips on her dresses had been moved when she was out.

Yet it was *she* who applied for a divorce on the grounds of her husband's unreasonable behaviour, saying that he had kicked a hole in the bathroom door, pulled the wires out of the telephone, and slapped her.

Judge Hunter, however, took the view that he didn't blame the husband, Mr Gerald Digby, who, he said, had been 'goaded to the limit' by the behaviour of a 'rather cold, utterly self-centred, and somewhat neurotic woman'.

Sir Richard Blake, 41, of Chichester, applied for a divorce from US jazz singer Bertice Redding, 49, in March 1983, saying that he had seen her only once since the wedding. He conceded that he had also had one letter.

She later said that he had flattered her during a whirlwind romance after they met in a restaurant. He promised to buy her a red rose and champagne every day, and she was happy.

> But when I looked at him in the church with his new clothes, it was a different Richard to the one I knew. He was the baronet and he wanted me to know it. I was disappointed. He really upset me, so I took my flowers and left.

*K*leenex millionaire James Kimberley found his six-year marriage to British model Roberta, 25, rather costly. After divorce papers had been filed, she claimed 'living expenses' of $250,000

a year—this in 1975—including flying lessons at $2,500 a week, clothes at $2,000 a month, and an 'entertaining allowance' of $40,000 a year. Mr Kimberley argued that, since their split, his wife's spending had 'increased dramatically'.

Chris Wastie was driven out of the family home . . . and lived in a wooden hut at the bottom of his wife's garden for 25 years, a divorce court heard in 1980. They never spoke.

The revelation came when Mrs Bridget Wastie, aged 68, of Charlbury, Oxfordshire, decided to formalize the split to qualify for a state pension. She was granted the divorce but scored something of an 'own goal'—the couple were ordered to split the property 50:50. In other words, he qualified for half her house . . . and she qualified for half his hut.

Mrs Patricia Smith, 36, of Hornsey, North London, sought a divorce in September 1968, after claiming that it was 'unreasonable' of her husband to object to her piano practice, even though this consisted of playing scales for up to nine hours at a time.

A couple of historic rulings: Mr Justice Karminski, in the London Divorce Court, decreed that, although a wife had thrown 'almost every form of domestic utensil' at her husband, this did not amount to cruelty. The crux of the decision: 'on almost every occasion, she missed.'

And in the same court Judge Clothier decreed

that a wife who demanded that her husband, on coming home from work each day, should kiss her first, then her sister, and then the cat 'had adopted a very unreasonable attitude'.

There are double standards in divorce cases, of course. Mrs Dorothy Dennis of San Francisco told a court that one night her husband, Colonel Chester I. Dennis, appeared in their bedroom with a 'fearsome-looking contrivance' in his hands. He wound it up and threw it under her bed crying: 'Bomb!'

It was, of course, just his joke. However, Mrs Dennis had refused to see the funny side and considered this grounds for separation. Colonel Dennis told her: 'You're got no sense of humour.'

The judge asked Colonel Dennis what he had to say for himself. He said the jape was merely in revenge for a stunt his wife had pulled the previous year when she had fastened a Fourth of July torpedo to the underside of the toilet seat. When he had sat down, it had exploded—not unnaturally causing some discomfort.

At the mention of this Mrs Dennis now burst into an uncontrollable fit of laughter. The judge turned to her and asked about the torpedo. 'It was very funny, very funny,' she said. 'Just a joke.'

15 We Will Bury You!

**I don't think I ever chose man-hating to be part of my life.
I think it chose me.**
Ingrid Bengis

Since the 'unknown' is stolen/hidden
know-ing, frozen and stored by the
Abominable Snowmen of Androcratic
Academia, Spinsters must melt these
masses of 'knowledge' with the fire of
Female Fury.
Mary Daly, 'Gyn/Ecology'

As for men, our escape from prison will
make the warder redundant.
Fanny Viner, 'In the Pink'

men denigrate our talk at their peril
but that's because they're in ignorance
of its power
our power
those previous few of us who see ourselves
as powerful
    serious
        and deadly
Astra

What we ask is nothing less than total
revolution, revolution whose forms invent
a future untrained by inequity,
domination, or disrespect for individual
variation—in short, feminist-anarchist
revolution. I believe that women have
known all along how to move in the
direction of human liberation; we only
need to shake off lingering male political
forms and dictums and focus on our own
anarchistic female analysis.
*Peggy Kornegger, US
anarcho-feminist*

Granny poured ink into a pillar-box.
Aunt Bertha cropped her hair.
Trudy chained herself to the bar in El
Vino.
I withdrew conjugal rights from my
husband.
It's been a week now and he still hasn't
noticed.
*Gill Butler 'Worse Verse', from the
'Sunday Times'*

16 The Queen of Spleen

The lips, the lips! He could French kiss a moose or blow a tuba
from both ends at the same time.
On Mick Jagger

She's the Number One for invective. The
Empress of Insult. The Queen of Spleen.
American comedienne Joan Rivers. Can we talk
here?

Did you ever date a football player? They
are *so* stupid. We'd get into an elevator.
He would press the buttons and look for
gum.

We went to a department store. It said
'Wet Floor'—he did.

He couldn't count to 21 unless he was
naked.

Prince Charles
His ears are so big he could hang-glide
over the Falkland Islands.

With those ears he can pick up cable TV.
He could play ping-pong without a bat.

He's so gay. He can't wait for his mother
to die so he can be queen.

John DeLorean
His cars come with 'snow' tyres as
standard equipment . . . The hood is a
spoon.

Michael Jackson
He's the guy that makes Liberace look like
Clint Eastwood.

Teddy Kennedy
When he lost to Jimmy Carter he said let
bygones be bygones—and offered to drive
him home.

Liberace
He is carrying Truman Capote's baby . . .
His big fantasy is to have Tom Selleck as a
proctologist.

Barry Manilow

Has he got a nose? . . . if he were on hard drugs, he could inhale Peru. When he retires he can work as a plough.

Robert Mitchum

If he'd just wear deodorant . . .

Fritz Mondale

He should have chosen Dolly Parton, not Geraldine Ferraro. Then they could have had three boobs at the White House.

Christopher Reeve

Who's interested in how many wires it took to keep him up? What everyone wants to know is . . . is he gay?

Burt Reynolds

[Face to face] Take off your toupee and blend right in.

Rod Stewart

He's got acne so bad that when he visits his dermatologist he has to be carried there on a stretcher. You could spend a year playing connect-a-dot on his face.

Stevie Wonder

Who's going to tell him that he's got a macramé plant-holder on his head?

17 A Kick Where it Hurts — Favourite Targets for Female Demolition: Literature and the Arts

> If I ever meet John Wells I should like to bite him.
> *Mary (Lady) Wilson on the stage show 'Mrs Wilson's Diary'*

*B*ecause of that devastating mix of fierce intelligence, unstoppable self-confidence and inability to be soft-soaped, women in the arts world are *the* enemy no man would choose to make. Yet every male actor, writer, playwright, musician and producer has at some time or another come up against this most fearsome of sex-war foes.

Probably the greatest example of an artistic kick where it hurts came at the Metropolitan Opera House, New York, in May 1982 during a performance of *Giselle*. That night the audience was astonished to see the celebrated dancer Gelsey Kirkland actually kick her partner Mikhail Baryshnikov—squarely and firmly up the backside.

The couple, who were known to be carrying on a private feud offstage, were starring in a performance by the American Ballet Theatre, of which Baryshnikov was the artistic director. In this capacity he had dismissed Miss Kirkland from the company two and a half years previously.

At her entrance she was given a rousing reception. It was only her second major New York appearance since being sacked. But soon it became apparent that she was doing her best to humiliate her leading man. During the second-act *pas de deux* things came to a climax when she suddenly unleashed upon him a rapid kick up the rear. The audience laughed and roared their approval.

As if this were not enough of a rebuke for the hapless Baryshnikov, he received another public put-down during the curtain calls. The fourth bow was in progress when someone delivered a bouquet of roses to Miss Kirkland. She plucked one out and held it invitingly towards a now confused Baryshnikov. However, as he moved forward to take it she suddenly backed away, then flung the bloom to the ground before storming off indignantly into the wings.

*O*ne of the most effective show-stoppers of all time came during rehearsals for Shaw's *Pygmalion* at Her Majesty's Theatre in 1914. One of the scenes called for the heroine, played by Mrs Patrick Campbell, to throw a pair of slippers at her leading man; Shaw was sensible enough to have the softest pair of velvet slippers provided for the purpose, 'for I knew that Mrs Campbell was very dexterous, very strong, and a dead shot'. Sure enough, at the crucial passage, the man in the firing-line—actor-manager Sir Herbert Beerbohm Tree—got the slippers delivered with great force—'and with unerring aim', said Shaw—straight in his face.

'The effect was appalling,' reported the author. 'He had totally forgotten that there was any such incident in the play; and it seemed to him that Mrs Campbell, suddenly giving way to an impulse of diabolical wrath and hatred, had committed an unprovoked and brutal assault on him.'

Tree collapsed in tears into the nearest chair, his morale shattered. And, according to Shaw, the scene in the play was thereafter ruined because Mrs Campbell had to make sure that her aim was suitably limp and completely off-target.

Mrs Patrick Campbell, in fact, used to terrorize writers and actors alike. When the young Basil Rathbone was engaged to play opposite her, he heard that she had told a friend:

Darling, I have no idea what his name is but he has got a face like two profiles stuck together.

Much later he met her and told her how upset he had been to be put down thus as a youth, when he had been extremely worried about his appearance. She hardly healed the rift, telling him:

Darling, you must forget all about it. Now you look like a folded umbrella taking elocution lessons.

*Q*ueen Mary delivered one of the most amusing literary put-downs in the 1930s when her husband, George V, was introduced to John Buchan, author of *The Thirty-nine Steps* and other classic thrillers.

The King said to him: 'I don't get much time for reading, but I do enjoy your books. Now, before you go, the Queen would like a word with you.'

Buchan moved on to talk to the Queen. She told him: 'The King doesn't get much time for reading, and I'm afraid when he does he reads the most frightful old rubbish.'

*T*o the musical world . . .

An objectionable old bore was once forcing himself on the famous New York diva, Miss Mary Garden. She was wearing the lowest of low-cut evening gowns. 'I can't imagine what's holding it up,' said the aged interloper.

'Possibly it's your age,' replied Miss Garden.
And the great lyric soprano Kiri Te Kanawa can show a mischievous sense of humour towards her male opposite numbers, according to her biographer, David Fingleton. He told how she was once singing the part of Carmen in New Zealand with Australian tenor David Smith in the part of Don José. At the point in the third act when Don José shoots a gun at some pirate, Kiri was off-stage. As Smith fired the first round, she lobbed onto the stage a dead duck, which landed right at the tenor's feet.

He only just managed to compose himself and carry on singing.

*T*he literary and arts worlds have produced some veritable classic victims of vituperation:

Nöel Coward
> His characters talk like typewriting.
> *Mrs Patrick Campbell*

E. M. Forster
> He never gets any further than warming the teapot . . . He's a rare fine hand at that. Feel this teapot. Is it not beautifully warm? Yes, but there ain't going to be no tea.
> *Katherine Mansfield*

André Gide
> If you've been married to the greatest writer in the world, you don't remember the little fellows.
> *Nora (Mrs James) Joyce*

Ernest Hemingway
> He didn't want to be nice. He just wanted to be worshipped.
> *Dorothy Parker*

Henry James
> An elephant that has picked up a pea.
> *Margot Asquith*

> All I can recall about him is my mother complaining that he always wanted a lump of sugar broken in two for his tea—and that it really was affectation, a small knob would do quite well.
> *Agatha Christie*

James Joyce
> The work of a queasy undergraduate scratching his pimples.
> *Virginia Woolf*

Charles Laughton
> [Face to face in the actor's dressing-room] Never mind, dear, I'm sure you did your best. And I'm sure one day you may be quite a good Macbeth.
> *Lillian Baylis*

Rex Reed
> Either at your feet or at your throat.
> *Ava Gardner*

Erik Satie
> He doesn't seem to have been quite normal.
> *Olga Satie (sister)*

George Bernard Shaw
> He kissed me once, but I derived no *benefit* from it.
> *Dame Edith Evans*

> If you give him meat no woman in London will be safe.
> *Mrs Patrick Campbell*

> I burn so with blushes at your confounded impudence, that I don't feel the cold . . .

May you freeze in that sea of ice in Dante's *Inferno*—I don't care.
> *Mrs Patrick Campbell again*

Lytton Strachey
> He seemed to have been cut out of very thin cardboard.
> *Edith Sitwell*

Gore Vidal
> It says a lot about the United States of America that such a foreign object as Gore Vidal can run for the Senate.
> *Jane Fonda*

Orson Welles
> Everything about him was oversized, including his ego.
> *Joan Fontaine*

18 The World's First Father-in-Law Jokes

He drinks a fair amount, you know. When he was in a car smash he lost so much blood that his eyes cleared up.

So who says no one makes jokes about fathers-in-law? As if you didn't know, a father-in-law is beer-swilling, billiard-playing, base ball-watching, boorish, bellicose, bilious . . . and boring. A quick trawl around some of my more aggressively feminist acquaintances produced the following:

He could have made the Cabinet . . . but he said no he couldn't find time to go to the DIY shop.

My father-in-law looks like a film star . . . King Kong.

My father-in-law's very temperamental. He's ten per cent temper and ninety per cent mental.

The new bridegroom was on the phone. He turned and shouted to his wife: 'How would you like to talk to father?'
    'Through a spirit medium' was the unkind reply.

On the way to the wedding the groom's father's eyes were so bloodshot he stopped three lanes of traffic.

He's *so* idle. Mind you, he took a pep pill once and ran all the way to the sofa.

My father-in-law is always proud to point out that he always makes the big decisions in the household, like whether the US and Britain should have a nuclear deterrent and whether

the US should invade Nicaragua. His wife makes all the small decisions, like where they should live, when they should buy a new car, and where they should go on holiday.

He's the original Deep Throat—his women friends call his 'Vesuvius' because he's empty inside and incredibly wide at the mouth.

He's inventive, though. He waters the lawns with whisky, saying the lawn will come up half-cut.

Tim's mother insisted Tim's father should put on a clean pair of socks every day. After a week he couldn't get his shoes on.

'I'm getting him a surprise for Christmas.'
　'What is it?'
　'A new tie.'
　'That's not much of a surprise.'
　'It is. He's expecting a bottle of Scotch.'

19 Classic Vitriol

For me he was never particularly mentally stimulating.
Britt Ekland on Rod Stewart

*W*omen have been adept at putting down their male counterparts for centuries. The *Golden Penny* in 1898 reported this:

> In the staid House of Commons, a very clever lady typewriter [typist] has been given a desk, salary and an assistant. When asked by Lord Salisbury to type a letter as she was about to leave she replied: 'It is not my place to work overtime for the Premier of England.'

*T*he undoubted female genius of the barbed *bon mot* was, of course, Dorothy Parker. Said she of an unnamed writer who, she considered, had an inflated reputation:

> He's a writer for the ages . . . for the ages of four to eight.

New York drama critic John McClain she slew with the observation:

> His body went to his head.

One of her best lines was to an actor who had just returned from London and who was putting on English affectations like pronouncing what the Americans call 'skedule', 'schedule':

> If you don't mind me saying so, you're full of skit.

While 'How can they tell?' was Miss Parker's query on being told that tactiturn former US President Calvin Coolidge was dead.

*O*ne of the best recorded put-downs came in the same era of the Algonquin from Peggy Leech, a friend of the celebrated journalist-wit Franklin Pierce Adams. Once, when the couple returned early from playing tennis, his shirt had come open at the neck to the extent that a curly black mass of chest-hair showed. Said Ms Leech:

> I see your fly is open higher than usual today.

After a spell when they plainly weren't on good terms, Barbara Walters, newly transferred from CBS, said in front of the cameras to the crusty Harry Reasoner, her ABC colleague:

> Unless you and I go on the air and

absolutely fornicate in front of everybody, people aren't going to think we're getting along.

Reasoner, who had been treating the divine Miss Walters with contemptuous indifference, was somewhat stumped for an instant reply.

Harry Cohen (Columbia boss)
> You had to stand in line to hate him.
> *Hedda Hopper*

Calvin Coolidge
> He looks as if he had been weaned on a pickle.
> *Alice Roosevelt Longworth*

David Frost
> He has risen without trace.
> *Kitty Muggeridge*

Clark Gable
> If you say 'Hiya, Clark, how are you?', he's stuck for an answer.
> *Ava Gardner*

Vittorio Gassman
> He used to grab me in his arms, hold me close—and tell me how wonderful he was.
> *(Ex-wife) Shelley Winters*

Barry Manilow
> Sings like a gnat stuck in a 6ft drainpipe.
> *Jean Rook, 'Daily Express'*

Robert Mitchum
> [Face to face] If you hadn't have been so good-looking you would never have gotten a picture.
> *Katharine Hepburn*

Al Pacino
> It doesn't even look like the same face any more. It's pasty, as if he'd vacated it.
> *Pauline Kael*

Arnold Schwarzenegger
> . . . has so many muscles that he has to make an appointment to move his fingers.
> *Phyllis Diller*

Rod Stewart
> He was so mean, it hurt him to go to the bathroom.
> *Britt Ekland*

Billy Wilder
> Long before he was Billy Wilder, he thought he was Billy Wilder.
> *Mrs Billy Wilder*

Terry Wogan
> That Tony Wogan was trying to get me to say I was jealous of my 22-year-old daughter. The nerve!
> *Raquel Welch*

20 Hell Hath No Fury: The Avengers

Sometimes when I drink too much, I can get extremely violent.
I go around BITING people. My director is wearing a coat of
chainmail right this minute.
Bette Midler

You don't have to look far to find spectacular examples to prove the old adage that 'hell hath no fury like a woman scorned'. Revenge in the sex wars is swift and sleek . . . and women have proved amazingly successful at meting it out. Sometimes they go further than mere words, of course, and the volume of water, wine and liquor poured over recalcitrant males would probably fill the Mediterranean.

Confirmed male superchauvinist Oliver Reed became victim of one of the first—and most historic—acts of celebrity retaliation, live on television, before 30 million US viewers, in the *Johnny Carson Show* in September 1975. Sparks flew as soon as Carson introduced Reed to Shelley Winters, a died-in-the-fur feminist. Soon the tension was mounting with exchanges like:

Winters: The English are kinky—they never talk about sex.
Reed: I agree, madam, we just do it.
Miss Winters then told Mr Reed his new moustache made him look like Hitler. He said that he was growing it for a film and that it was only four days old. 'I suppose that proves I'm not very virile,' he said.

Miss Winters shot back: '*Now* I remember you!'

Reed countered: 'There is no doubt why, madam, you awoke next morning with a pencilled moustache on your . . .' (The next word was bleeped out by the censors.)

Miss Winters then walked off. Mr Reed poked fun at her, saying 'So much for Women's Lib' and sounding off about a woman's place being in the kitchen.

Miss Winters then made a surprise reappearance.

Mr Reed, like the gentleman he is, stood up—only to have the actress pour a pint of whisky over his head.

'I'm not indignant, I'm not!' claimed Reed afterwards. 'This is indicative of a lot of show-business ladies.'

Unemployed waitress Sally Nicholson, 25, knew what to do when she found her 45-year-old lover in bed with another woman . . . she put on her stiletto heels.

But it was what she did next that was unforgettable: she clambered up onto the roof of his Rolls Royce and did a tap dance, causing £1,700 worth of damage.

Mr Andrew MacFarlane, defending her, told Bath magistrates in June 1984: 'It was an act of passion.'

In December 1967 the *Guardian* reported an incredible incident on the backbenches when the Health Minister, Mr Kenneth Robinson, uttered what were described as 'anti-feminist sentiments'. Said the paper: 'There followed a loud "hear, hear" from Dr John Dunwoody on the benches behind him. This, in turn, was followed by an even louder "thwack"—the sound of Dunwoody's head being smitten by a rolled order paper wielded by Mrs Gwyneth Dunwoody sitting just behind.'

Actress Pamela Stephenson caused something of a stir when she poured cold water over the head of a BBC presenter, Kenneth Robinson, during the live Radio Four programme *Start the Week* in July 1982. He called her a 'very vulgar little person', to which she responded that he was 'a silly old fart'.

On another occasion in October 1982, Miss Stephenson sent one of the most inventive of gifts from an actress to a critic. Jack Tinker of the *Daily Mail* received an exquisitely gift-wrapped cowpat. She said: 'I hope he enjoyed it.'

Perhaps the most famous recent act of feminine retribution came at a party in June 1983 when Anna Ford, a presenter sacked by TV-am, threw a glass of Chablis over her former boss, MP Jonathan Aitken, drenching his £300 suit. Miss Ford described her aim as 'pretty good' and added: 'If I had been a man I would have punched him in the nose—he can count himself very lucky. It might have been better if the wine had been red.'

Mrs Teri Shields got her own back on one of the men pestering her daughter Brooke at the Cannes Film Festival in 1979. She bit the ear of a waiter who was trying to ingratiate himself with her daughter. 'I think she is more determined than pushy,' explained her daughter.

And a report in *Reveille* claimed that police in Corpus Christi, Texas, once answered an emergency call from a distraught housewife who invited them indoors and told them to arrest her husband for being drunk. When told that he had a perfect right to be drunk in his own home, she threw him out into the street.

The police then arrested him.

*O*ne of the most widely publicized examples of a woman celebrity getting her own back was when Texan model Jerry Hall decided to show boyfriend Mick Jagger just what she thought of his philandering. In her autobiography *Tall Tales* she tells how she kept finding another woman's hairpins in Mick's bed . . . and decided to get even. She took off with Robert Sangster, the millionaire racehorse owner. The Rolling Stone was soon on the phone begging her to return to him.

'She did it just to get in the newspapers,' he moaned afterwards.

*A*fter being jilted, a department-store assistant from Stockholm had the perfect plan for vengeance upon all men: she put itching powder into every pair of socks she sold. Success went to her head, however. She was found out after she had tried to persuade girls in another department to put itching powder into every pair of underpants they sold.

Juan-Alfonso Serra, of Bogota, Colombia, didn't give his wife much of a clothing allowance. Her revenge was original. In March 1983 she went out into the street, stripped off all her clothes, and paraded in a one-woman nude demonstration. She told passers-by: 'I haven't a thing to wear.'

Spurned Bordeaux housewife Claudine Naudier put advertisements in sex magazines inviting people to orgies at the home of her ex-husband and his new young wife. She was fined £1,000 by local magistrates for causing a nuisance, but said: 'It was worth it.'

Rita Lewis, 51, of Hastings, Sussex, in March 1985 punished her husband for staying late at the pub. She dialled 999 and complained to the police that the landlord was serving after hours. In due course the landlord was fined £50 by local magistrates and sacked from his job.

Mrs Lewis was unrepentant. She said: 'I was fed up with my husband coming back from there drunk.'

A 'snooker widow' from Maidstone, Kent, wreaked her own justice on the club which took up all her husband's time—by stealing in and calmly ripping 13 tables with a knife. She stormed into the club while members were chalking their cues and lunged at the green baize, sending reds, greens, blacks and blues scattering in all directions and causing £4,500 of damage.

She left only one table at Maidstone Snooker Club undamaged before rushing off into the night.

'We just couldn't believe it,' said a male member. 'It is an unusual way to stop someone playing.'

Police said they were having trouble finding the culprit. All the men who had been there on the night were 'too frightened' to give a description.

21 Woman's World, Man's Place

The Superior Being

Of course there's no such thing as a totally objective person, except Almighty God if she exists.

Antonia Fraser

I refuse to consign the whole male sex to the nursery. I insist on believing that some men are my equals.

Brigid Brophy

Once a woman is made man's equal, she becomes his superior.

Margaret Thatcher

Women have dominated men for so long, I don't understand all this yipping.

Lucille Ball

Man in his Place

There are men I could spend eternity with, but not in this life.

Kathleen Norris

The man is only her priest, living in fear and trembling of her displeasure. His sole function is to perform the various ceremonies that centre around the sacred object.

Pauline Reage, 'The Story of O'

My husband and I count for 10; I am the one, he is the zero.

Mrs Massey-Harris, US feminist

You see an awful lot of smart guys with dumb women, but you hardly ever see a smart woman with a dumb guy.

Erica Jong

I require only three things in a man. He must be handsome, ruthless and stupid.

Dorothy Parker

I've lived with Paul for two-and-a-half years. He was passed on to me by my sister. She said 'Do you want him?' and I said, 'All right.'

Tracy Ullman

He was my boyfriend for six months, and he never forgot it. It must have been bliss for him.

Bette Midler on ex-manager Aaron Russo

22 A Kick Where it Hurts — Favourite Targets for Female Demolition: Politics

One of the things that politics has taught me is that men are not a reasoned or reasonable sex.
Margaret Thatcher

*H*ave you ever wondered why men hate women coming into politics? It's because, of course, it hurts. Hear this on President Reagan from Democratic Congresswoman Pat Shroeder in 1983:

He has achieved a political breakthrough—the Teflon-coated presidency. He sees to it that nothing sticks to him. He is responsible for nothing—civil rights, Central America, the Middle East, the economy, the environment. He is just the master of ceremonies at someone else's dinner.

Lesley Quiller of Dunedin, Florida, was a forgetful sort. So much so that she could not help, it seems, crashing into her garage doors. Her response was to have a portrait of Ronald Reagan (whom she loathed) painted on them. Said she: 'It hasn't stopped me crashing into the doors, but now when I do I feel a helluva lot better about it.

According to the 'People' column (Jan 29), Ronald Reagan liked the movies more around the time he was in them. I liked the President more when he was in the movies.
Letter in 'International Herald Tribune' (Hannah Baker, Bures-sur-Yvette, France)

A competition in the London *Evening Standard* in March 1983 to find 'Britain's Wettest People' was dominated by female entrants . . . and male poll-toppers, led by Mark Thatcher and Michael Foot. First prize was won by a lady from Charlwood, Surrey, who said Mark Thatcher's getting lost in the Sahara

'gave a new meaning to the phrase "drip dry"', while a young woman from Wimbledon proclaimed Willie Whitelaw 'the Wishee-Washee of political panto'.

*L*yndon Johnson used to tell the story of his teenage daughter coming home and saying: 'Daddy, as an outsider, how do you feel about the human race?'

> The President asked me what I thought about Mrs Gandhi's loss in the elections. But I told him: 'No comment.' He said, 'But I'm your son, the President of the United States.' And I said: 'It's still no comment.'
>
> *'Miz' Lillian Carter*

Pity poor Tony Benn. He boasts of a strong radical family background, yet when his niece Frances went up to Oxford in 1982 she immediately joined . . . the university's Conservative Association. Her stated view of her uncle pulled no punches:

> To say he's naive sounds like a personal insult and makes me sound like a woman of the world . . . it's fairer to say he's . . . straightforward.
>
> I think he comes over as very aggressive—he evades questions and tends to sidestep issues.
>
> When he appears on television you think: 'Who is this sour fanatic?'

*B*ut what of the lady who became the world's most successful female politician? How did she treat her male colleagues? Well, she may have knocked Neil Kinnock for six by saying he 'didn't have the guts' to condemn violence in the miners' strike, but she displayed a female-chauvinist streak towards her own colleagues, too. Early in her premiership, Mrs Thatcher lined up her Cabinet for a formal visit to the Palace to be presented to the Queen.

She inspected them to make sure they were spick and span, naturally. But then—oh, horrors, Sir Geoffrey Howe was wearing . . . *brown shoes*. Not any common or garden brown shoes, either, but a particularly scuffed pair of Hush Puppies.

'You will have to change them,' she trilled to Sir Geoffrey. 'What size are you?'

Luckily for all concerned the answer was size 10—the same as Denis takes—and a borrowed pair was swiftly produced in which Sir Geoffrey could squeak up the Palace steps.

Another time, in June 1983, during the final stages of their election campaign, Mr and Mrs Thatcher arrived at Manchester Airport. Denis Thatcher, for some reason, got separated from the rest. 'Where's Denis?' asked a supporter.

'I expect he's trying to get some duty frees,' quipped his wife.

More barbed still. On being told in February 1985 by a Channel-4 TV producer that a previous interviewee on the show, Cecil

Parkinson, had asked for a fee to donate to his favourite charity, the Prime Minister responded, with no pause for thought: 'I hope that it was for the Save the Children Fund.'

The most disloyal and damaging member of the whole government.
Barbara Castle on James Callaghan

Perhaps the greatest and most accurate insult-hurler of the political world was Lady Violet Bonham-Carter, Herbert Asquith's daughter. Over a period of three decades, not a statesman escaped her thunderbolts. She had a mischievous wit, shown at her first meeting with Lord Haldane. She greeted him as an old friend. He was puzzled and asked where she had seen him before.

'Why, in *The Nonsense Book*, of course,' she replied.

She said later: 'His kind of pneumatic bulk, plenoid outline and twinkling benignity was exactly like the famous old man in Edward Lear's book.'

Clement Attlee

Mr Attlee reminds me of a flea-bitten grey. How often has one seen a poor horse in summertime, beset by flies and hornets, protect itself from them with its tail. But in Mr Attlee's case, it's the tail that's doing the stinging.

Aneurin Bevan

Such a gift horse to his opponents that it would be ungrateful for us to look him in the mouth.

Winston Churchill

He looks at the world through bloodshot spectacles.

Sir Stafford Cripps

He has a brilliant mind—until he makes it up.

Sir Stafford is a man who can turn on the light—but never the heat. I have heard him compared to a poker, with its occasional warmth.

Bonar Law/Lloyd George

We are asked to choose between one man suffering from sleeping sickness, and another from St Vitus Dance.

David Lloyd George

Mr Lloyd George has split one party, and there is evidently some chance of his wrecking another. Perhaps, before many months have passed, he will try to build a raft—out of the splinters of both.

Harold Macmillan

One long cock-a-doodle-do of self-congratulation.

Quintin Hogg

It might have been better for his party had he used his bell more frequently—to drown his voice.

On the Tory ex-peer's much publicized 'bell-ringing for a Conservative victory' campaign.

Harold Wilson

I liked Sir Alec's little joke about the fourteenth Mr Wilson—but I am not sure he is right. I think Mr Wilson is the fourteenth in a long line of computers. If he were a racehorse, the stud-book would say: By Computer, Out of Electronic Brain.

*I*n recent years two women have emerged as challengers to inherit Lady Violet's crown: journalist Jean Rook and Sir Harold Wilson's former secretary, Marcia, Lady Falkender.

Jean Rook's Best Barbs

Her choice comments on the leading figures of the 1983 election included:

Michael Foot

Pathetic, outdated, washed up. He has rot, and the tragedy is this once brilliant orator is beginning to talk it.

His eyes, hair and gestures are wild, his voice echoes a thunder long spent. A shambling, at times rambling old man,

lashing himself into a raging tempest against what he must know is his fate.

Foot is no longer Worzel Gummidge. He is a white-haired, storm-shaken Lear. You wish they would mercifully remove him from the stage.

Ted Heath
Behaves like a spoiled brat who'll pound the whole lot of them into jelly if he can't sit at the head of the table.

Roy Jenkins
Looks like a claret-cheeked little Toby jug who doesn't measure up.

Enoch Powell
You can smell political death on him.

Norman Tebbit
He fascinates me like a totally charmless snake.

Willie Whitelaw
Smacks of tuck and midnight feasts in the dorm. He's as old-fashioned as a half-sucked bullseye or a yellowing copy of *Boy's Own*.

Murder by Marcia, Lady Falkender
The best from her column in the *Mail on Sunday*:

John Biffen
Increasingly spoken of as the Tory Right's dark horse, but I'm afraid he is more like a dark sheep to me—he makes me nod off.

Michael Foot
The Jekyll and Hyde of politics.

John Selwyn Gummer
We all felt happy for young Gummer when we read in our newspapers: 'Small-bore gold medal win for Britain.' How disappointing then to discover that this had to do with rifle shooting and nothing whatever to do with him.

Roy Jenkins
Often out of touch . . . add to this his general aura of having stepped straight out of an After Eight mints advertisement and it is possible to see why his success with the Labour Party faithful was wafer thin.

Neil Kinnock
The perfect cabbage-patch politician. Springing from apparently nowhere, warm, lovable, and with an adoption certificate in his hands ready to be planted down in the best of nurseries.

23 Classic Cuts

Dr Christiaan Barnard
>The man is too old.
>>*Lolita Moreno, Miss Switzerland, to whom he had proposed*

Warren Beatty
>An emotional cripple—for life.
>>*Michelle Phillips*

>The incurable philanderer.
>>*Britt Ekland*

Richard Burton
>The pimply, blockheaded star.
>>*Joan Collins*

Marlon Brando
>Old and flabby . . . He had a little complex . . . Kept pulling the curtains when he got changed . . . All the time, watching his make-up.
>>*Maria Schneider*

Prince Charles
>Anodyne.
>>*Margaret Thatcher*

Sebastian Coe
>Too much in love with himself.
>>*Linda Greeves, tennis starlet*

Christopher Dean
>Almost part of the furniture.
>>*Jane Torvill*

James Dean
>He nice but only a boy.
>>*Ursula Andress*

Bob Dylan
>A young neurotic.
>>*Joan Baez*

Clark Gable
>A lousy lay.
>>*Carole Lombard*

David Hicks
>Just plain boring.
>>*Janet Street-Porter*

Leslie Howard
>Old Womanish.
>>*Mary Morris*

Howard Hughes
  He couldn't understand where the fourth wall was.
  Mary Astor

Richard Ingrams (of *Private Eye*)
  A coward and a bully.
  Diana Dors

Richard Nixon
  The best potato-masher one could wish for.
  His mother, Hannah

Robert Redford
  Virtually sexless.
  Erica Jong

Frank Sinatra
  Just a saloon singer.
  Barbra Streisand

Lord Snowdon
  A failed architect.
  Princess Margaret

---

24 A Last Word on Men

*S*ome final sex-war sloganizing:

WHEN YOU'VE ADAM, DON'T THEY MAKE YOU EVE?

MY HUSBAND MADE ME HAPPY BY ADDING SOME MAGIC TO OUR MARRIAGE—HE DISAPPEARED

JESUS WAS A TYPICAL MAN—THEY ALWAYS SAY THEY'RE COMING BACK BUT THEN YOU NEVER SEE THEM AGAIN

FOR FEMININE PROTECTION EVERY DAY . . . USE A HAND-GRENADE

CAN YOU BEAT MY RECORD OF 71 MEN?—YES, IF YOU SUPPLY THE WHIPS

I'M GLAD I AM A WOMAN
I'M GLAD THAT I AM FREE
BUT I WISH I WERE A LITTLE DOG
AND MY HUSBAND WAS A TREE

Suggestions for Further Reading

*I*t would be too space-consuming to list here the myriad of newspapers, magazines and books which have aided the preparation of this volume. It may be helpful to the (female) reader who would like to delve into the subject of sex wars more fully, however, to list the works likely to best whet the appetite.

Radical Feminism

Bengis, Ingrid: *Combat in the Erogenous Zone*, Wildwood, 1973

Daly, Mary: *Gyn/Ecology*, The Women's Press, 1979

Quiet Rumours: An Anarcha-Feminist Anthology, Dark Star (Rebel Press), 1983

Mythology

Graves, Robert: *The Greek Myths* (2 vols.), Penguin, 1960

Guerber, H. A.: *The Myths of Greece and Rome*, Harrap, 1938

Monaghan, Patricia: *Women in Myth and Legend*, Junction Books, 1981

Female Tyrants

Millan, Betty: *Monstrous Regiment: Women Rulers in Men's Worlds*, The Kensal Press, 1982

Suffragettes and Politics

Fulford, Roger: *Votes for Women*, White Lion, 1976

Phillips, Melanie: *The Divided House*, Sidgwick & Jackson, 1980

Raeburn, Antonia: *The Militant Suffragettes*, Michael Joseph, 1973

Vallance, Elizabeth: *Women in the House*, Athlone Press, 1979

Insults

Celebrity Research Group: *The Bedside Book of Celebrity Gossip*, Prince Paperbacks, New York, 1984

Tester, Mary: *The Wit of the Asquiths*, Leslie Frewin, 1976

Biography

Falkender, Marcia, Lady: *Downing Street in Perspective*, Weidenfeld and Nicolson, 1983

Gabor, Zsa Zsa: *My Story*, Arthur Barker, 1961

Graham, Sheilah: *My Hollywood*, Michael Joseph, 1984

WHAT'S HE DOING IN MY BOOK!